6.94

Map of Oregon counties and cities:

Astoria
CLATSOP
COLUMBIA
St Helens
TILLAMOOK
WASHINGTON
Hillsboro
MULTNOMAH
Portland
Tillamook
YAMHILL
Oregon City
McMinnville
CLACKAMAS
Hood River
HOOD RIVER
The Dalles
WASCO
Moro
SHERMAN
GILLIAM
Condon
MORROW
Heppner
Pendleton
UMATILLA
UNION
La Grande
WALLOWA
Enterprise
Dallas
POLK
SALEM
MARION
Fossil
WHEELER
Baker
BAKER
Newport
LINCOLN
Corvallis
BENTON
Albany
LINN
JEFFERSON
Madras
Prineville
CROOK
GRANT
Canyon City
Eugene
LANE
Bend
DESCHUTES
Vale
Roseburg
DOUGLAS
COOS
Coquille
KLAMATH
LAKE
Burns
HARNEY
MALHEUR
CURRY
Grants Pass
JOSEPHINE
Gold Beach
JACKSON
Medford
Klamath Falls
Lakeview

The New

Enchantment of America

OREGON

By Allan Carpenter

 CHILDRENS PRESS·CHICAGO

ACKNOWLEDGMENTS

For assistance in the preparation of the revised edition, the author thanks:
JACQUELIN M. GETTIS, Travel Information, Oregon State Highway Division; POLLY EYERLY, Curator of Education, Portland Art Museum; and BOB BRUCE, Director of News Bureau, University of Oregon.

American Airlines—Anne Vitaliano, Director of Public Relations; *Capitol Historical Society*, Washington, D.C.; *Newberry Library*, Chicago, Dr. Lawrence Towner, Director; *Northwestern University Library*, Evanston, Illinois; *United Airlines*—John P. Grember, Manager of Special Promotions; Joseph P. Hopkins, Manager, News Bureau.

UNITED STATES GOVERNMENT AGENCIES: *Department of Agriculture*—Robert Hailstock, Jr., Photography Division, Office of Communication; Donald C. Schuhart, Information Division, Soil Conservation Service. *Army*—Doran Topolosky, Public Affairs Office, Chief of Engineers, Corps of Engineers. *Department of Interior*—Louis Churchville, Director of Communications; EROS Space Program—Phillis Wiepking, Community Affairs; Charles Withington, Geologist; Mrs. Ruth Herbert, Information Specialist; Bureau of Reclamation; National Park Service—Fred Bell and the individual sites; Fish and Wildlife Service—Bob Hines, Public Affairs Office. *Library of Congress*—Dr. Alan Fern, Director of the Department of Research; Sara Wallace, Director of Publications; Dr. Walter W. Ristow, Chief, Geography and Map Division; Herbert Sandborn, Exhibits Officer. *National Archives*—Dr. James B. Rhoads, Archivist of the United States; Albert Meisel, Assistant Archivist for Educational Programs; David Eggenberger, Publications Director; Bill Leary, Still Picture Reference; James Moore, Audio-Visual Archives. *United States Postal Service*—Herb Harris, Stamps Division.

For assistance in the preparation of the first edition, the author thanks:
B.L. Simmons, Director, Curriculum and Instructional Services, State Department of Education; Mark O. Hatfield, former Governor; Forest Cooper, State Highway Engineer; Dennis Clark, Head, Travel Information Division; Gladys B. Price, Indian Festival of Arts, Inc.

Illustrations on the preceding pages:
Cover photograph: Yaquina Lighthouse on the Oregon coast, TWA
Page 1: Commemorative stamps of historic interest
Pages 2-3: View from Otter Crescent, Lincoln County, Travel Information, Oregon State Highway Division
Page 3 (Map): USDI Geological Survey
Pages 4-5: Portland Area, EROS Space Photo, USDI Geological Survey, EROS Data Center

Project Editor, Revised Edition:
 Joan Downing
Assistant Editor, Revised Edition:
 Mary Reidy

Library of Congress Cataloging in Publication Data

Carpenter, John Allan, 1917-
 Oregon.

 (His New enchantment of America)
 SUMMARY: Presents the history, resources, famous citizens, and points of interest in the Beaver State.
 1. Oregon—Juvenile literature.
[1. Oregeon] I. Title. II. Series.
F876.3.C28   979.5   78-13955
ISBN 0-516-04137-1

Contents

A True Story to Set the Scene

THE CRUISE OF THE DEAD

The silent figures of many Indians dotted the bluffs. They had come to watch one of the strangest processions ever to take place. Their ancestors were sailing out to sea.

The year was 1856, a troubled time in Oregon's history. Indian unrest and growing nationwide disturbances were upsetting not only the people of Oregon, but the whole country.

A young lieutenant had been sent by the United States government to help keep order in Oregon. He was Phil Sheridan, who later became one of the famous generals in the Civil War.

Sheridan planned to build a blockhouse as a military strongpoint and decided that the south shore of Yaquina Bay was ideal for his fortification. The Indians, however, strongly objected.

The proposed location of the blockhouse was the final resting place for Indian dead of many generations, carefully laid out in ceremonial death canoes. The goods the Indians believed the dead would need were placed in the colorfully decorated burial canoes. No place was more sacred to the Indians.

Many pow-wows were held. At last, the Indians reluctantly gave in to the military pressure and agreed that the ground could be cleared for the fortification. But they feared moving their dead and so the Americans said that they would undertake the eerie task themselves.

The soldiers pushed the burial canoes into the surf. As the Indians and the whites watched, the craft slipped out into the ocean, bearing the bodies of Indians in a long single line.

Some of the Indians who watched that grim funeral procession may have foreseen the even more grim future of their race. Once Indians had controlled the whole great continent; but their influence soon would fade almost as completely as their ancestors had slipped away into the vast ocean.

Opposite: Memories of the early peoples are still honored in such displays as the Comcomly Canoe and the Astor Column, in Astoria.

Lay of the Land

Most people would call Oregon a western state and also a northern one. After all, it is on the Pacific coast, and much of it lies as far north as Minnesota, Michigan, New Hampshire, or even Maine. Yet Oregon occupies the precise center of the United States.

If you could fit the entire country into one enormous box, thousands of miles long and wide, you would find that Point Barrow, Alaska, would just touch the northern edge. Cape Prince of Wales, Alaska, would reach to the western side of the box, while Quoddy Head, Maine, and the southern beaches of Hawaii would come to the eastern and southern edges of the box.

The true center of this gigantic area would be found in the forests of China Cap Mountain, a few miles northeast of the ghost town of Pondosa, in northeast Oregon. This is now the geographical center of the United States. It moved halfway across the continent when Hawaii and Alaska became states.

BY THE SEA, BY THE BEAUTIFUL SEA

Oregon stretches for nearly 300 miles (483 kilometers) along one of the most varied coastlines on earth. Many important landmarks dot this shore.

The world's highest sand dunes are found south of the Umpqua River. In the Coos Bay area, the jumbled rocks of the shore show what happened centuries ago when ancient earthquakes twisted the rocks into an untidy clutter.

Huge rocks jut up from the sea, including such landmarks as Tillamook Head and Otter Crescent. Another landmark is Haystack Rock, on Cannon Beach, the third largest rock monolith in the world. Smaller rock formations rise along most of the coast, like a natural skyline.

Opposite: Haystack Rock at Cannon Beach, Cape Kiwanda.

The sea has cut and carved into the land and sometimes splashes into spectacular displays of surf and foam. At Whaleshead Beach, a peculiar formation of the rock makes the tide spout like a giant whale. Another spot is the Devil's Churn, where the tides surge and writhe.

THE RIVERS OF WATERS

Into the spectacular beaches flow the waters of many unusual rivers. The legend of the origin of the greatest of these is a classic of American folklore.

It seems that the enormous, mythical lumberjack, Paul Bunyan, had just hitched his mountainous blue ox, Babe, to the plow when the animal went on some kind of rampage. It tore away from its master and went lumbering across the country toward the sea, pulling the great plow behind it.

By the time the enraged Paul caught up with Babe, the ox had reached the seashore. The plow had dug such a tremendous furrow straight through the mountains that not even a Bunyan could fill it up. Gradually the furrow filled with water, and today we call it the Columbia River.

The actual origin of the Columbia is only a little less spectacular. The Cascade Mountains and coastal range acted like a great dam, holding back the waters of a vast inland sea that once covered much of present-day Oregon and Washington. Waters of this sea began seeping through the mountains to cut an opening to the ocean. Over the years, the water cut deeper and deeper until the Columbia River was formed and the inland sea drained away. Near where it meets the sea at Astoria, the Columbia is seven miles (eleven kilometers) wide.

In some places the waters cut down two thousand feet (six hundred meters) into solid rock to make the great gorge of the Columbia River. Oregon, in fact, is a land of spectacular gorges. One of the deepest clefts in the face of the earth is Hell's Canyon, slashed into the rock by the Snake River. For forty miles (sixty-four kilometers) this jagged gash drops to an average of six thousand feet (eighteen hundred meters) below the rim on either side. This canyon is almost a thousand feet (three hundred meters) deeper than the Grand Canyon of the Colorado River. Hell's Canyon is on the border between Idaho and Oregon.

The Snake River forms a major part of Oregon's eastern boundary. Not so spectacular, but more important to Oregon, is the Willamette River. Its valley supported the earliest and most extensive development of the state. Other Oregon rivers included in the United States Geographical Survey of principal rivers are the Deschutes, Klamath, and Owyhee. Some additional Oregon rivers are the Rogue, McKenzie, Umpqua, Suislaw, Metolius, and Clackamas. The Clackamas is one of the most beautiful streams in the northwest.

Hell's Canyon (left), one of the deepest clefts in the face of the earth, was carved out by the action of the Snake River.

13

Beautiful Crater Lake was formed when volcanic Mount Mazama erupted and the mountain walls collapsed, leaving a huge cavity which gradually filled with water. It is the deepest lake in the United States.

The junction of the North Umpqua and Little rivers at Glide, Oregon, is one of the few places where two rivers meet head on. Usually one flows into the other.

Altogether, Oregon enjoys fifteen thousand miles (twenty-four thousand kilometers) of rivers and streams.

BLUE MIRRORS: THE LAKES

One of the best known of Oregon's lakes is Crater Lake. Actually, Crater Lake is not in a crater. Its basin is called a caldera. At one time the highest mountain in Oregon was Mount Mazama. About seven thousand years ago, volcanic Mount Mazama erupted. So much lava and ash were thrown over the countryside that almost the whole interior of Mount Mazama was consumed. By the time the eruption was over, the mountain walls had become so thin they eventually collapsed, leaving a great cavity where there once had been a mighty mountain. Gradually the huge hole filled with water, and Crater Lake was born.

Crater Lake has neither an inlet nor an outlet, yet it remains at about the same level year in and year out. It never varies more than 4 to 6 feet (1.2 to 1.8 meters) in depth, in spite of the 50-foot (15-meter) snows that blanket the region. Crater Lake is the deepest lake in the United States—1,996 feet (599 meters). For a long time, in fact, it was thought to be bottomless.

Upper Klamath Lake is the largest body of water within the state. Other lakes include Devils, Crescent, Diamond, Malheur, and many lakes formed by dams.

OTHER NATURAL FEATURES

The Wallowas and the Blue Mountains are neighboring ranges in eastern Oregon. To the west the Cascade range is crowned by Oregon's highest point, Mount Hood, 11,245 feet (3,374 meters) high. Mount Jefferson, at 10,495 feet (3,149 meters), is Oregon's second-highest peak. Between the Cascades and the Wallowas is a high basin area, which runs diagonally into southeast Oregon, where it meets northern Nevada in dry and desolate country.

The third of Oregon's roughly parallel mountain ranges is the Coast Range. Between the Coast Range and the Cascades is a great valley, occupied in large part by the Willamette River and its tributaries.

Abert Rim, in Lake County, is the largest earth fault in North America. It is two thousand feet (six hundred meters) high and thirty miles (forty-eight kilometers) long.

IN TIMES PAST

Much of Oregon's land has been covered at one time and another with shallow seas. These have come and gone as the earth's surface has changed over the centuries. Mountains were thrust up by great forces. One of these was the volcano. The power at work in volcanic action is shown by the quantity of lava rock and volcanic ash still to be seen.

In the case of Mount Mazama, enough material was thrown onto the surrounding countryside to build a seventeen-mile (twenty-seven kilometer) cube. After the collapse of the mountain, there was still enough volcanic energy left to push up the bit of land that is called Wizard Island. The region called the Pumice Desert resulted from the flood of lava pouring out of Mount Mazama.

The largest lava beds in the world are found in the region of the Three Sisters Mountains near the McKenzie River. Malheur Cave is a lava cone ½-mile (.8 kilometer) deep.

Evidence of the heat beneath the earth's surface can still be seen in Oregon. Volcanic smoke has been observed on Mount Hood in modern times. Oregon has many hot springs; the world's largest continually flowing geyser is found at Lakeview, spouting as high as forty feet (twelve meters).

In Oregon's past was great cold as well as violent heat. Much of the state was covered with sheets of ice during the glacial periods. As

16

they moved, the glaciers changed the face of the land, filling valleys and gouging out lake beds. Wallowa Lake is one of the glacier-formed bodies of water, and the shores of the lake are fine examples of what is called glacial moraine.

Not all of Oregon's glaciers have vanished. Nine glaciers still cling to the slopes of Mount Hood, continually replenished by the vast snowfalls. The Three Sisters glacial area near Bend is well known.

Winter scene in the Mount Ashland ski area.

Footsteps on the Land

Not too far from the town of Lexington, archaeologists have discovered an ancient stone sepulcher. From the evidence found here, the experts feel that this may have been a Mayan burial place. How Mayans found their way from their homes in far-off Mexico to northern Oregon is just one of the many mysteries of prehistory.

However, there are some written records that survived from prehistoric times. In many parts of Oregon today there is found a kind of ancient writing, called pictographs—generally line drawings of people, animals, or objects, carved or painted on the rocks or bluffs. The exact meaning of these writings has not been deciphered, although some of them are fairly easy to understand. Good examples of pictographs are found at Picture Gorge and Condon-Day State Park. It is possible that at some future time the key to these writings may be found, and our knowledge of Oregon history will be extended thousands of years.

Judging from the items that prehistoric people left behind in Oregon, authorities feel that human beings have been in the region for at least ten thousand years. It is probable that they first arrived far earlier than that.

FROM THE EGGS OF THE THUNDERBIRDS: THE INDIANS

The modern Indians of the Oregon region have been known almost since the first European ships sailed along the shores. The Indians told the early Europeans some interesting legends about how they came to be in this land.

One of these legends tells of the great and powerful Thunderbird, perched on its aerie high atop Saddle Mountain. When its eggs were about ready to hatch, the Thunderbird rolled them down the steep

Opposite: A University of Oregon archaeology team
uncovers the story of prehistoric life in southeastern Oregon.

slopes. End over end they bounced, protected by their thick shells. When they reached the valley, they hatched the first Indians.

A multitude of Indian tribes and subtribes inhabited the Oregon region. Mountains, forests, and bluffs kept the small groups confined very much to their own areas. There were many languages and variations of languages, especially in the western sections, so that it was difficult for members of different groups to communicate with one another. When Europeans began to come in, the Indians developed a language called Chinook. This was a combination of Hawaiian, English, Spanish, French, and Indian. The Chinook language helped the Indians to trade with the Europeans.

Some of the many Oregon Indian groups include Athapascan, Salishan, Karok, Calapooyan, Sahapatian, Atfalati, Rogue, Cayuse, Coquille, Klamath, Shasta, Takelman, Wasco (or Wacopam), and Chinook. There were thirty-six different branches of the Chinooks alone.

Early explorers found the Chinook Indians living in luxury on the wonderful salmon that now bear their name—the huge Chinook. Many tribes gathered for an annual ceremony of the salmon to pray for the fish's favor.

The Chinook and other western tribes traveled in huge canoes hollowed out of red cedar trees. Sometimes these were as many as sixty feet (eighteen meters) long. It took many months, even years, to hollow out some canoes. Often they were decorated with beautiful carved designs.

The western Indians wove clever fishing nets of tough grasses and generally wore clothing made of animal skins. Certain western Indians were skillful in the use of more than two hundred plants and herbs of the region. They lived in enormous cedar plank lodges and carved their totems of the same fragrant cedar.

Lewis and Clark wrote in their journal: "The Indian women wear a short petticoat of the inner bark of the cedar, which hangs down in loose strings nearly as low as the knee."

The Indians of eastern Oregon formed their houses from the earth itself. Eastern Oregon Indians were more nearly like the Indians of the Great Plains. Tribes and groups of the east mingled more freely

Left: Kwakiutl, a double mask of the Northwest Coast Indians. Below: The Pendleton Roundup recalls a proud Indian heritage.

than those of the west. Before the coming of *sayapoo,* or white people, Indians of many tribes gathered in the Grande Ronde Valley each summer to renew friendships, to trade, and to show one another their crafts and horses—all differences forgotten.

To the south, the Shasta and Takelman groups lived in winter wickiups (dwellings much like tepees), wore clothing of animal skins, and hunted with short bows.

FIRST EXPLORERS

Only fifty years after Columbus had discovered the New World, Spanish explorers were moving up the western coast of America. An exploring party under Juan Rodríguez Cabrillo made many discoveries in California. After Cabrillo died during the voyage, the party continued up the coast under the leadership of Bartolomé Ferrello. It is generally thought that in 1543 the explorers must have been the first Europeans to see the shore of what is now Oregon, but the exact northern limit of their discoveries cannot be determined. England's Sir Francis Drake may have reached Oregon's southern coast in 1579.

In 1603 Martin d'Augilar sighted a prominent feature of the coastline and called it Cape Blanco, a name it still bears. This was the first place in Oregon to be named by Europeans.

For a hundred and seventy years, while the eastern American colonies were developing, Oregon lay as it had for centuries. If a few adventurous captains came into contact with the Oregon region during the period, they had little effect.

Sometime during this period the Indians of eastern Oregon discovered a strange and wonderful new animal. It had been brought to the Western Hemisphere by the first Spaniards and quickly spread to far regions. This was the horse, and horsemanship soon became an important part of Indian life.

A Spanish explorer, Bruno Heceta, wrote on August 17, 1775: "On the evening of this day I discovered a large bay. . . . The currents and eddies caused me to believe that the place is the mouth of

22

some great river.'' Those same currents kept Captain Heceta from entering the bay and actually seeing that great river, which we know today as the Columbia. Nonetheless, Heceta is credited with its discovery, and on the basis of that discovery, Spain laid claim to the Oregon country.

English explorer Captain James Cook sailed along the Oregon coast in 1778 and gave Cape Foulweather its name. It was not until ten years later that the American Captain Robert Gray of the *Lady Washington* became the first white person known to have set foot on Oregon soil—in what is now Tillamook County. When he entered Tillamook Bay, some of his men came in conflict with the Indians. One of them was killed in the first skirmish between whites and Indians in Oregon history. Because of this tragedy, Captain Gray called the place Murderers' Harbor.

Gray returned in another ship, the *Columbia,* and sailed up and down the Oregon coast several times. On May 11, 1792, he decided to risk his boat in the extreme currents at the opening of Heceta's ''large bay'' to become the first to enter the great river of the West.

The *Columbia* sailed fifteen miles (twenty-four kilometers) up the river. There the Indians came down to trade. Two huge salmon could be bought for one small nail. The rate for prime beaver skins was two spikes. On the shore of the river, Gray laid in a large supply of furs, including 150 of the rare and precious sea otter, for which merchants in China paid as much as a hundred dollars each.

The river of Gray's discovery had been called the River of the West—or by the Indian name, the *Ouragon*—for many years. Captain Gray named the river Columbia in honor of his ship, but for many years people continued to call it the Ouragon, or Oregon. Poet William Cullen Bryant wrote in *Thanatopsis* in 1817, ''Where rolls the Oregon, and hears no sound save its own dashing.'' The poem soon spread the name Oregon over the whole region, and the name of Gray's ship gradually again became associated with the river.

Shortly after Gray left the river, one of the vessels in the British fleet of Captain George Vancouver also braved the fierce currents and entered the Columbia. This ship was the *Chatham,* under Lieutenant William R. Broughton.

Broughton sailed up the Columbia for 100 miles (160 kilometers), discovering the mouths of the Willamette and Sandy rivers. When he sighted "a remarkable mountain clothed with snow," he gave it the name Mount Hood in honor of English Admiral Lord Samuel Hood. He also named a spot on the north shore of the Columbia in honor of his commander, Vancouver.

TRADERS AND TRAVELERS

By 1800 American ships controlled most of the fur trade on the northwest coast. So many of the ships were from New England that the Indians began to call all Americans "Bostons." A complete trading voyage lasted three years. The "stately clippers of the China trade" would leave New England ports, sail around Cape Horn, and up to the Oregon coast. There they would trade their beads, trinkets, blankets, and a few tools or other items with the Indians for the precious sea otter, beaver, and other furs. After taking on water and supplies, they would sail for China, usually stopping at the Hawaiian Islands for more supplies. In China teas, spices, silks, and other goods of the Orient were acquired in exchange for furs. Sometimes as much as $250,000 was made in one voyage.

By 1820, however, the trade had dwindled because more money could be made by whaling in the Atlantic.

Due to the discoveries of Gray and Vancouver, both England and America claimed the Northwest. When the United States purchased the vast Louisiana Territory, President Thomas Jefferson sent an expedition to travel overland, exploring the new territory. They were to reach the Pacific Ocean, if possible.

Toward the close of one of the most important and dramatic journeys in our history, the explorers, headed by Captain Meriwether Lewis, assisted by Captain William Clark, reached the portion of the Columbia River that borders present-day Oregon. There were thirty-three members in their party, including Sacajawea, their famous Indian woman guide. Only one member of the party died on the journey, and that was a natural, not a violent, death.

A state capitol mural pictures the Lewis and Clark expedition.

To carry them down the western rivers, the Lewis and Clark party followed the Indian example and made five canoes by hollowing the western red cedar.

Where the Columbia once swirled over Celilo Falls, Lewis and Clark portaged. But when they reached the fantastic place where the river used to turn on edge and squeeze itself through a crack only 150 feet (45 meters) wide, they boldly shot through in their sturdy canoes, like arrows flying from Indian bows. This location later was called the Dalles.

It became clear to the travelers at this point in their journey that the Indians had been in contact with the outside world. They saw the kettles, blankets, and trinkets given by the traders for the Indian furs. Already the native people of Oregon were harder to deal with than the Indians of the interior had been.

After portaging past the cataract of the Cascades, Lewis and Clark reached the region of ocean tides and thought they were almost at their goal—not realizing that tides sweep up the mighty river for almost 160 miles (256 kilometers). The remainder of their voyage was calm until on November 7, 1805, they saw the thundering Pacific for the first time.

Close to the coast, they built Fort Clatsop on Young's Bay. It would serve as their headquarters for the winter of 1805-1806. One of the principal reasons for choosing this site was the unusually good hunting; plentiful elk provided a sure supply of meat. They also had easy access to the ocean, which they needed for salt-making.

One of the most exciting events of their stay occurred when a great whale was washed up on Cannon Beach. Captain Lewis wanted its blubber, so the whole party, including Sacajawea, hurried down to the beach.

Lewis and Clark built Fort Clatsop on Young's Bay. It has been recreated at the Fort Clatsop National Memorial (below).

In March, 1806, they began their return journey. Not one trading boat had come to the Columbia during their stay, although the Indians were expecting traders.

On their return, Lewis and Clark found the mouth of the Willamette River. It is not clear how they missed it on their downstream voyage. They predicted that the region might one day support fifty thousand people. Today it is the site of the city of Portland, and hundreds of thousands inhabit the area.

Before they left Oregon, Lewis and Clark gave certificates to the Chinook and Clatsop chiefs, telling of their just and hospitable treatment. One historian describes "the faithfulness, honesty, and devotion of the Indians when entrusted with any charge, as the care of horses or canoes. This character of the Indians was so marked that one can hardly avoid the conclusion that the subsequent troubles with the Indians were due largely to abuse by the whites."

Although this was not the first journey overland across the American continent—Alexander Mackenzie had crossed what is now Canada in 1793—it caused a sensation throughout the world. Most historians agree that the journey of Lewis and Clark was of great importance in the claims of the United States on what came to be called the Oregon Territory—Oregon, Washington, and parts of Idaho, Montana, Wyoming, and British Columbia.

FORTUNES IN FURS

The wealthy American John Jacob Astor had established many profitable fur stations in wilderness outposts. He and his partners decided to form the Pacific Fur Company and set up headquarters in the Oregon Territory. Two partners, Duncan MacDougall and David Stuart, went by boat, the *Tonquin,* around Cape Horn. They stopped at the Hawaiian Islands for a crew of native Kanaka laborers and arrived at the mouth of the Columbia in March, 1811. In crossing the sandbar of the Columbia, seven men were killed, including one of the Kanaka. With much wailing, his comrades, according to custom, put a bit of food and some tobacco under his arm, a dab of

27

lard on his chin, and buried him in the sands. John Astor's new settlement had its first grave before it actually came into being.

For the new headquarters, MacDougall chose a site not far from Fort Clatsop. They immediately began construction of what they called Fort Astoria. This was the beginning of the first permanent white settlement in Oregon.

While this work went on, Captain Jonathan Thorn went out with the *Tonquin* to do some fur trading. Thorn was a fierce and disliked man. When one of the Indian chiefs asked for a higher price for a fur than Captain Thorn was willing to offer, the captain pushed it into his face. The next day the Indians came back and massacred the captain and the whole crew of twenty-three. Before he died, one of the crew set fire to the powder magazine and blew the ship and the Indians into the air.

In July, David Thompson of the Canadian Northwest Fur Company came down the river, greatly disappointed that he was too late to establish his company at the mouth of the Columbia.

Two members of the Astor party, Alexander Ross and David Stuart, went up the Columbia and established an American trading post on the middle river at the Okanogan. During the first six months they took in fifteen hundred fine beaver pelts. They estimated they made sixty-four dollars on every dollar's worth of goods they traded.

Meanwhile, another Astor partner, Wilson Price Hunt, had been traveling overland from St. Louis to reach the mouth of the Columbia. Hunt chose a difficult route and very nearly lost the entire party. At last, most of them reached the Columbia and floated down in canoes. Passing Tongue Point, they were thrilled to see the stars and stripes flying over the only spot where it had yet been raised on the Pacific coast. They had reached Astoria at last.

Six men of the Wilson Hunt party had been too sick to go on and had been left with the Indians. Two of these men, John Day and Ramsey Crooks, recovered enough to start westward again later. They were captured by Indians, stripped of all clothing, and robbed of all possessions. After wandering until they were almost dead, they were met by a rescue party near the mouth of the Umatilla.

John Day never recovered his health. He lost his mind and died not long after reaching Astoria. A number of landmarks in Oregon still bear his name. One of these is the John Day River, along which he and Crooks traveled for so many weary, barren miles. Later, the other four men who were left with the Indians were found, although no one had expected to see them alive again.

The War of 1812, between Britain and the United States, changed matters on the Columbia. When news reached the Astor partner MacDougall that a British warship was coming to capture Astoria, he quickly sold out to the Canadian Northwest Company for much less than the value of the property. When the Treaty of Ghent ended the war in 1814, Astoria (called Fort George for a time) was held by the British, and Astor was compelled to leave it in Northwest Company hands. Later, in 1817, President Monroe sent a warship to Astoria and seized the area.

The Convention of 1818 prevented further strife. According to this treaty, both English and Americans were to have equal rights to trade and make settlements in the Oregon Territory. The Americans continued to hold Astoria, but the Northwest Company was left undisturbed.

For ten years the Northwest Company controlled the fur business of the Columbia, until it merged with the Hudson's Bay Company. During those years the business was not very well managed.

In 1824 the powerful governor of the Hudson's Bay Company, Sir George Simpson, came 2,000 miles (3,200 kilometers) on foot and by canoe to see his company's new outpost. With him was the company's chief factor, or manager, Dr. John McLoughlin. These were both remarkable men.

Realizing that the Indians and other people around the fort would be much impressed by appearances, they arrived at Astoria with bugles blowing. A bagpiper in full kilt played the company onto the shore, his whining notes resounding through the wilderness. Each man was perfectly shaved and cleanly dressed, and each wore a feather in his cap.

Dr. McLoughlin stayed on to be the company's governor in the Oregon Territory. He held this post for more than twenty years, and he ruled like an emperor in his huge domain. The period of his power has been called the McLoughlin Era.

He left Fort Astoria and for his new headquarters built Fort Vancouver on the north bank of the Columbia, almost opposite the mouth of the Willamette, in what is now Washington State. Later, outlying forts were set up in the farthest reaches of the territory.

The rich trade in furs expanded. Sawmills were set up to cut lumber for export. Salmon were salted and exported. British ships visited the Columbia frequently to bring supplies and haul away the rich products of the new Oregon outpost. The Hudson's Bay Company was richer and more powerful than many of the real empires of its day.

Into this territory came many a wandering traveler and trader, including Jedediah Smith, Captain Benjamin L. E. de Bonneville, and Nathaniel Wyeth. Wyeth tried to establish a business on Sauvies Island, but he could not compete with the Hudson's Bay Company and sold out to them.

THE MISSIONARIES

Wyeth had brought with him four dedicated missionaries, led by the young Methodist Reverend Jason Lee. The story of their "call" to the mission field is one of the most unusual in American history.

In 1832 four Indians, starving from their long journey from the Far West, appeared in St. Louis. They are generally described as being from the Flathead tribe, but one authority states that three were Nez Percé and the fourth a Flathead. General William Clark was superintendent of Indian affairs at St. Louis. He treated the four Indian guests well and finally learned that they had made their trip across the continent to get a copy of the white people's "Book of Life."

Two of the older Indians died in St. Louis. The other two finally started back to their homes. The famous artist George Catlin was on the same boat with them on the way up the Missouri River. He wrote, "When I first heard the object of their extraordinary mission across the mountains, I could scarcely believe it; but, on conversing with General Clark on a future occasion, I was fully convinced of the fact." Catlin painted pictures of the two Indians, and they were listed in his mammoth collection.

It is not clear how these Indians heard about the Christian religion; possibly they learned from some of the traders or trappers. Their touching story, however, had a remarkable effect on the American public. The president of Wilbraham College asked, "Who will respond to go beyond the Rocky Mountains and carry the Book of Heaven?" The call of these Indians "stirred the church as it has seldom been stirred into activity."

The first of those who responded was Reverend Lee. With his nephew, Daniel, he set up a mission station and school near present-day Salem in 1834.

Later, Reverend Lee tried to get the United States to make Oregon a territory officially. The effort failed, but Lee was not discouraged. He returned to the East by the overland route in 1838. In 1840 he brought back by ship a party of fifty-one pioneers. This was the largest group of settlers ever to come into the region, and they quickly found farms in the Willamette area.

Jason Lee was not the only missionary in the Oregon country. Dr. Marcus Whitman and Reverend H. H. Spalding made the long trip overland with their wives in 1836. This was the first overland journey ever made to the West Coast by white women. It took more than four months and covered 2,200 miles (3,520 kilometers). The Whitmans had only recently been married.

Dr. Whitman set up a mission in what is now Washington, and Reverend Spalding did the same in western Idaho.

WAGONS OF THE PIONEERS

In the years that followed, a few more pioneers came in to settle, but the American government considered Oregon a desert and took little interest in obtaining the rights to it. Dr. Whitman became alarmed that the United States might give up its rights in the Oregon

Territory and leave England in possession. In October, 1842, he hurried overland from his mission to St. Louis. His perilous winter journey attracted great attention.

In Washington, Dr. Whitman conferred with Secretary of State Daniel Webster and later with President Tyler and his cabinet. They agreed not to oppose the passage of a large wagon train to Oregon, which the doctor already had helped to promote. Dr. Whitman hurried back to Missouri and found that an enormous wagon train had left. Close to a thousand people had loaded their goods into 120 wagons and plodded off, accompanied by fifteen hundred horses and cattle.

Dr. Whitman caught up with the party before it reached Fort Hall in Idaho. The Hudson's Bay Company leader at Fort Hall tried to convince them that no wagons could be taken over the last thousand miles (sixteen hundred kilometers) between Fort Hall and the Willamette Valley. Dr. Whitman, however, had made the journey with his own wagon, so the travelers took his advice and went ahead.

In spite of the roughest wagon road anyone had ever seen, they made it to the Columbia. For miles the Indians came to view the incredible caravan. The Indians called the pioneer wagons *Chik-Chik-Shaile-Kikash*. This was their way of trying to imitate the sounds that the wagons made as they trundled along. Nothing like this movement of people had ever been attempted before in the area.

Once they had reached the river, they hoped to make flatboats and glide down the Columbia with little trouble the rest of the way. It was not to be so easy. They could not get through the Cascades at the Dalles. Some of the flatboats overturned, drowning members of the party.

On one of the boats that overturned was a young boy. He was carried for almost two miles (three kilometers), often held under water by the current, buffeted and tossed by the rapids. Finally he was tossed onto a slippery ledge. Just then he saw a young man from the same boat being swept by. The first boy grabbed him and brought the young man to the ledge. There was a sheer cliff above them, which they could not climb. The first boy decided to plunge back into

Capitol mural of Chik-Chik-Shaile-Kikash,
the Indian name for pioneer wagons.

the river and make his way across a reef to the other shore. When he had almost made it, he saw that his companion had been afraid to try. The boy came back and helped his friend across, and they both made it to safety.

When the party could not sail the Cascades of the Columbia, they tried to cut a road around the rapids; but their supplies gave out, and it appeared that they would starve.

Just then news of the party reached Dr. McLoughlin at Fort Vancouver. "A thousand people?" he exclaimed. "What manner of men are these that scale the mountains and slide down the rivers?"

Dr. McLoughlin knew that if such a large immigrant party ever landed in Oregon and were able to establish themselves there, it probably would hasten the end of the control of his Hudson's Bay Company in the region. Yet he could not let anyone starve.

At the historic Champoeg gathering (shown at right in a House Chambers mural) settlers met in May, 1843, to decide whether the Oregon Territory would be governed by America or Canada.

"Man the boats," Dr. McLoughlin cried, and in fifteen minutes every boat was on the water. They shot out on their errand of mercy and arrived at the Cascades none too soon. Years later some of the women of the party recalled the scene, sobbing, "God bless Dr. McLoughlin."

Soon the overland boats began to come down the Columbia to Fort Vancouver. Dr. McLoughlin stood on the river bank for days "personally supervising the arrival of the immigrants as if they had been his own invited guests."

Before they went on up the Willamette, most of the immigrants received supplies and seeds for planting the coming crop from Dr. McLoughlin. Those who could not pay were given supplies on credit. Before long, the men who had been left to drive the cattle over the Cascade Mountains arrived in the Willamette Valley.

Not long before the first flood of newcomers arrived, the earlier settlers in the Willamette Valley had taken a historic step. The people gathered at Champoeg in May, 1843, to vote on whether the

Oregon Territory would be governed by America. The settlers of Canadian descent were against, the Americans for. An old account tells of the historic meeting: " 'Let us divide and count,' the Secretary said. . . . The lines marched apart, swayed a moment, hesitated at deadlock then . . . two Canadians crossed to the American side." It was just enough. The vote was fifty-two in favor of American rule, fifty against.

Though the government formed at Champoeg was not official, it has been called the first American government west of the Rocky Mountains. It was decided there would be no taxes; all revenue would be raised by voluntary gifts and subscriptions. The first time this was tried, the voluntary gifts amounted to only $80.50. That was hardly enough to govern the vast Oregon Territory, so taxes were levied.

During the winter of 1843-1844, after the arrival of the first great tide of immigrants, a village sprang up at the falls of the Willamette. Oregon City began to prosper. Its ambitious settlers created a library, a lyceum, and other evidences of civilization. The first Protestant church west of the Rockies, a Methodist church, was built there.

But this 1843 immigration was only the beginning of an impressive mass movement. The road this first group blazed, with the help of Dr. Whitman, became the famous Oregon Trail. Despite the dangers of Indians, famine, disease, weather, and flood, they came by the thousands. The ruts made by their wagons were cut so deep that they may be seen even today in some places. And at the end of the trail lay rich, fertile Oregon.

For a time the travelers continued to go by land to the Dalles and transfer to boats for the rest of the journey. But in 1845 S.K. Barlow and William Rector cut the Barlow Road through to the upper Willamette Valley. One historian notes: "Canyons, precipitous rocks, morasses, sand-hills, tangled forests, fallen trees, criss-crossed and interlaced with briars and vines and shrubbery of tropical luxuriance, such as no one can appreciate who has not seen an Oregon jungle—those were the obstructions of the Barlow road. But they were vanquished in 1846 and from that time on the immigrants made this the regular route to the Willamette Valley."

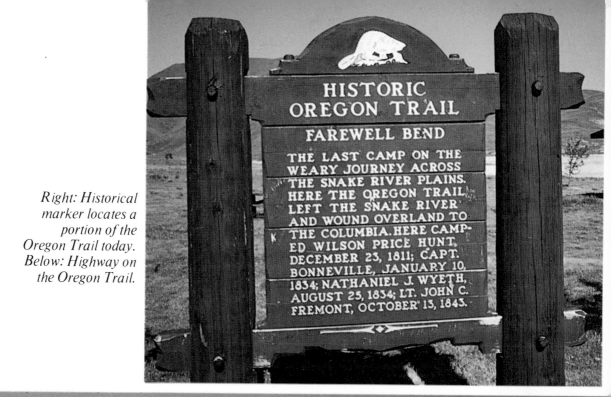

Right: Historical marker locates a portion of the Oregon Trail today. Below: Highway on the Oregon Trail.

HISTORIC
OREGON TRAIL

FAREWELL BEND

THE LAST CAMP ON THE WEARY JOURNEY ACROSS THE SNAKE RIVER PLAINS. HERE THE OREGON TRAIL LEFT THE SNAKE RIVER AND WOUND OVERLAND TO THE COLUMBIA. HERE CAMPED WILSON PRICE HUNT, DECEMBER 23, 1811; CAPT. BONNEVILLE, JANUARY 10, 1834; NATHANIEL J. WYETH, AUGUST 25, 1834; LT. JOHN C. FREMONT, OCTOBER 13, 1843.

FIFTY-FOUR FORTY OR FIGHT

The coming of so many settlers was displacing the great Hudson's Bay Company. Dr. McLoughlin agreed to accept the terms of the provisional government created at Champoeg.

But many of the British wanted warships and troops to hold the territory for Britain. They said the journeys of Cook, Vancouver, MacKenzie, and Broughton had established their claim to the region. The Americans pointed to Gray, Lewis and Clark, and Astoria. Most important, they could show the thousands of Americans settled there, already operating under a self-established government that claimed to be American. There were no large numbers of British settlers to offset this claim.

Feelings in the American East grew strong. The election of 1846 gave rise to the slogan "Fifty-four Forty or Fight." The American people would be satisfied with nothing less than placing their boundary at 54° 40′ north latitude.

Just when war seemed inevitable, both sides agreed to a compromise. The border between the United States and Canada was established at 49°, where it has remained to the present time, and the treaty was proclaimed on June 15, 1846. Prime Minister Robert Peel of Britain said proudly, "The governments of two great nations have by moderation, by mutual compromise, averted the dreadful calamity of war."

Oregon became part of the United States. Dr. McLoughlin resigned as governor for the Hudson's Bay Company and moved to Oregon City, where he had claims on a large amount of property.

Before the United States could organize its new lands, the Mexican War flamed up, and Oregon was left to continue in much the way it had.

INDIANS STRIKE BACK

While all these changes were going on, the Indians grew more uneasy. "The poor Indians are amazed at the overwhelming number of Americans coming into the country,'' wrote Narcissa Whitman, wife of Dr. Whitman.

Some of the Indians in the territory had originally come from the East; Delaware, Iroquois, Cherokee, and others knew from first-hand experience that the coming of the settlers meant the loss of lands, freedom, and frequently life itself for the Indian.

The Indians were hardly afraid of the Hudson's Bay Company. The company wanted to keep the land much as it had always been, so that the fur-bearing animals would continue to flourish. The traders brought in no large groups of settlers to push the Indians from their land. The company kept the Indians supplied with kettles, blankets, and other trinkets the Indians had come to value.

In addition, Dr. McLoughlin was viewed by the Indians almost as a god. He had an ability to treat the Indians in just the right way to command their respect. During the more than twenty years that Dr. McLoughlin ruled with an iron hand as governor of the Oregon Territory, not a single serious Indian disturbance occurred. This is a remarkable record of peaceful relations.

By 1846, however, peace had come to an end. Dr. McLoughlin no longer ruled. Sickness had claimed many Indian lives. The Indians felt that the settlers had brought this sickness to them, and they were right: the settlers did carry diseases that were previously unknown to the Indians.

The Indians turned on their former friend, Dr. Marcus Whitman. They said he was a medicine man and accused him of bringing sickness and death to the Indians. In November, 1847, the Indians murdered Marcus and Narcissa Whitman, who had devoted much of their lives to Indian welfare, and massacred thirteen others at the mission. They also took some forty-five women and children captives.

THE TERRITORY OF OREGON

The provisional government of Oregon was faced with fighting an Indian war without help from the United States. It had forty-three dollars in its treasury and no militia; but it borrowed from the Hudson's Bay Company and the Methodist mission and managed to send five hundred men to put down the Indian uprising. The conflict became known as the Cayuse War.

The provisional government of Oregon sent trapper Joe Meek overland to Washington to bring word of their difficulties to the federal government. This Oregon pioneer and the message he brought about the Whitman massacre created a sensation in the East.

Congress had been considering a bill to create an Oregon Territory. It had been long delayed by those who wanted to find some means of permitting slavery in Oregon, or at least of keeping another free state from being created. At last, however, on August 13, 1848, Congress passed the bill creating Oregon Territory. This huge area included all of present-day Oregon and Washington and parts of Idaho, Wyoming, and Montana, regions drained by the great Columbia River.

A rising young legislator named Abraham Lincoln was asked to become the first governor of Oregon Territory. He gave careful consideration to the honor. It would have given him a great deal more power and influence than he had at that time. However, he declined with thanks.

General Joseph Lane accepted the post of territorial governor, and Joe Meek became the United States marshal. The "technically illegal but efficient" provisional government under Governor George Abernathy came to an end. Oregon had become the seat of the first official American government west of the Rockies.

As the Cayuse War drew to a close, five of those who were responsible for the Whitman massacre were captured. They were sentenced to hang. Marshal Joe Meek was assigned to be their executioner. He used an Indian tomahawk to cut the ropes and dropped them to their deaths on the gallows.

Yesterday and Today

PROSPERITY AND PERILS

The discovery of gold in California brought good times to Oregon. Many settlers left their homes in Oregon and hurried south to the gold fields. Being so close to the scene of the strike, many Oregonians were able to make rich claims and come back to Oregon bearing sacks of gold or gold dust. Oregon farmers and merchants also benefited from the California gold rush. The hordes of people coming to California created a fine market for Oregon livestock and produce.

The Donation Land Law of 1850 provided that a man and wife could claim a full section of land—640 acres (256 hectares). Wives came into great demand in Oregon among unmarried men who wanted to be able to claim the largest amount of land possible. Many eligible girls, as young as fourteen and fifteen, were quickly wooed and wed in time to claim a full section.

In 1850 the population of Oregon was 13,294. By 1855, only five years later, it had risen to more than 40,000.

In 1853 a new Oregon Territory was created, reducing the former area to that south of the Columbia River and the forty-sixth parallel. The area north of this boundary became the Territory of Washington.

California did not have a monopoly on gold. Prospectors began to find it in southwestern Oregon, particularly in the area around Jacksonville. A year or so after the California strike, a mining boom developed in Oregon.

The Indians resented the intruders who were ripping up their ancestral hunting grounds. So began the Rogue River War, 1855-1856. Many settlers and gold seekers were killed.

One isolated settler's home that was attacked belonged to George Harris. When the attack began, Harris was wounded. His wife did

Opposite: "The Oregon Pioneer" statue at the state capitol building in Salem

not even know how to load or fire a rifle. Before he died, Harris was able to show his wife how to use a gun. For nineteen hours the desperate but courageous woman held off the Indian attack to save herself and her children. The United States cavalry appeared just in time to save them. Today Mrs. Harris's tombstone may still be seen in the old Jacksonville cemetery, bearing an inscription of her valor.

STATEHOOD AND STRIFE

In November, 1857, Oregon approved a constitution and applied for statehood. The new Oregon constitution excluded both slaves and free blacks. The growing unrest over the question of slavery had an effect, even in faraway Oregon. The pro-slavery people fought the admission of a new free state with all their resources. At last, however, on February 14, 1859, Oregon became the thirty-third state of the United States of America.

The news of this event traveled overland by express from St. Louis, the end of the telegraph lines, to San Francisco. It was brought by steamer to Portland and hurried on horseback to Salem. It took more than a month for the news of statehood to reach the capital. State officers had been elected almost a year before; at last John Whiteaker knew that he could legally claim to be the first governor of the state of Oregon.

Oregon was to have its first opportunity to vote for a president in the critical election of 1860. The brilliant Edward Dickinson Baker stumped the state for the Republicans and their candidate, Abraham Lincoln. It is said that largely because of Baker's efforts the state voted for Lincoln and sent Baker to the United States Senate.

In 1861, the man who had refused to become the governor of Oregon Territory only a few short years before—Abraham Lincoln—became president of a bitterly divided country. Almost as he took office the Civil War erupted.

Baker resigned from the Senate to enter the army. When he was killed in a charge at Ball's Bluff, he became one of the first Union officers to give his life for his country.

42

Senate Chambers mural, Statehood, Admitted to the Union February 14, 1859.

The war itself did not reach Oregon's boundaries, although Fort Stevens was built in 1864 to guard against the possibility of Confederate gunboats entering the Columbia River. The major disaster to sweep Oregon during the wartime period was a natural one. The flood of 1861 in the Willamette Valley was the worst in the history of the region. It completely swept away the historic settlement of Champoeg.

Oregon was not without fighting in this period, however. The Modoc War in southern Oregon and northern California was an especially fierce Indian conflict. It is sometimes said to have started because of a raid by John C. Frémont on an Indian village. Fort Klamath was built, not far from Crater Lake, for protection during the Modoc War.

To the north, also, the Indians were restless. Lewis and Clark had felt that the Nez Percé Indians were the most honest and intelligent of all those they met on their trip. In a treaty of 1855, the Wallowa country had been reserved for the Nez Percé, under their famous Chief Joseph. As more and more settlers came in, however, the pressure to take over the Indian lands became almost overwhelming.

In 1863 the treaty was amended. The new terms called for the Nez Percé to leave the Wallowas (which had been guaranteed them forever) and take up life on a reservation. Neither Chief Joseph nor his son, Young Chief Joseph, recognized this treaty, and they continued to occupy their ancestral lands.

Old Chief Joseph died in 1871. His grave is near the north end of Wallowa Lake. In 1877 Young Chief Joseph finally agreed to leave his Valley of the Winding Waters and take his people to the reservation. Before the Indians left, settlers stole a large number of Indian horses.

Their beautiful spotted Appaloosa horses were the most precious possession of the Nez Percé. Although they had lived peacefully with the settlers for almost seventy years, the Nez Percé now decided to go to war. Joseph was sure that they were not strong enough to make a stand, so he and about five hundred of his people began a retreat toward Canada, where they hoped to find safety in the wilderness.

Joseph's four-month journey of more than 1,000 miles (1,600 kilometers) has been called one of the most masterful retreats in military history. More than twelve battles were fought during the retreat; the Indians escaped four different armies. Finally they reached the Bear Paw Mountains of Montana, only a few miles from the Canadian border. Starvation, fatigue, and cold forced the Indians to give up on October 5, 1877. The war with the Nez Percé is said to have been the last great Indian war in the United States.

MODERN STATE IN A MODERN AGE

Although the first transcontinental railroad was completed to California in 1869 and many railroads had been built in Oregon, it was not possible to go across the continent from Portland entirely by rail until 1883. Until that time wagons and stagecoaches provided the only wheeled transportation for connections to the East.

At the turn of the century, a number of events captured the attention of Oregonians. One of the most important was a new method of more-direct government by the people, often called the Oregon

System. In 1902 the initiative and referendum system of direct legislation was adopted. The primary election method of selecting candidates for office was started in Oregon in 1904. By 1911 the Oregon primaries included a presidential preference.

In 1908 Oregon adopted a system through which its citizens could recall officials who appeared not to be serving their best interests.

One of the first events that attracted travelers in large numbers to Oregon was a world's fair, the first ever to be held on the West Coast. This was the Lewis and Clark Centennial Exposition, held in 1905, just a hundred years after those two travelers pioneered the long trail to Oregon.

Also in 1905 a canal and locks were begun around Celilo Falls in the Columbia to make that river more navigable.

The western states were considerably more advanced than other states in recognizing women's rights. In the early 1900s only the states of the West granted the vote to women. Oregon joined this group in 1912.

During World War I, the Third Oregon Infantry was the first National Guard regiment in the country to be mobilized and ready for service. The mushroom growth of shipyards, especially in the Portland area, helped to provide Uncle Sam with much-needed transportation across the seas.

In 1933 work began on a project that people had dreamed about for generations—a dam across the Columbia, just below the Cascades. This dam was to be named for Captain Benjamin L.E. de Bonneville, a pioneer western explorer and trapper.

By 1938 Bonneville Dam was transmitting power. The dreaded chute of the Columbia became a placid pool. Deep-water ships could pass through the locks and travel the river as far as the Dalles.

The dam provided one of the first great tests of fish "ladders"—a kind of stair-step arrangement to lead migrating salmon up and around dams by easy stages.

World War II came to Oregon shores on June 21, 1942. A Japanese submarine fired several five-inch (thirteen-centimeter) shells at Fort Stevens. This was one of the few occasions when war reached the shores of the United States.

The growth of Oregon shipbuilding was even more startling in this war than it had been in World War I. Eleven hundred and seventy-four ocean vessels were built in the Portland-Vancouver area during World War II.

The Forty-first Oregon National Guard was the first major army unit to enter the South Pacific after Pearl Harbor.

In 1962 another "war" came to Oregon, but this time it was a war of the elements. The storm named Frieda was the worst in Oregon history. Portland suffered winds up to 116 miles (186 kilometers) per hour; wind velocity reached 170 miles (272 kilometers) per hour at Mount Hebo. At Salem, the winds caused more destruction than any other natural disaster ever had done. Great damage was done also to forest and timber lands.

By July, 1963, the Oregon population had reached 1,856,190—more than 40 percent growth since 1940. During the 1970s the state discouraged the influx of new residents. The growth rate stabilized at about 9 percent. That decade also saw Oregon's emergence as a conservation leader. It was the first state to outlaw nonreturnable beverage containers (in 1972) and to ban fluorocarbon aerosol cans (in 1977).

In the old days Dr. John McLoughlin and Nathaniel Wyeth were talking about the future of Oregon. Wyeth said, "Our policies are opposed. Yours is to perpetuate savagism, to keep Oregon as a game preserve, a great English hunting park. Mine would be to fill it with civilized people."

"How can they get here, Mr. Wyeth? Even India is not so far. Oregon is the very end of the world, a whole year's voyage around Cape Horn or Good Hope. Shut off by rock-ribbed mountains, deserts, savages, the ocean, how can they get here?"

"Overland from the United States," answered Wyeth.

Dr. McLoughlin laughed, "When you have leveled the mountains, cultivated the desert, annihilated distance, then and not before."

If he could return today, the good doctor would be amazed. The mountains in effect have been leveled, the desert cultivated, and the distance annihilated; Oregon is now only hours away from anywhere.

Natural Treasures

TIMBER-R-R!!!

Oregon cherishes the largest stands of virgin timber in all the world. More than thirty million acres (twelve million hectares) of the state are covered with standing forests, and Oregon ranks third among the lumber states. This amount of timber would completely cover Rhode Island, Delaware, Connecticut, Hawaii, New Jersey, Massachusetts, and New Hampshire—with five Rhode Islands left over.

The people of Oregon have not always cherished this wealth. The Indians used to set fires every year to clear away the undergrowth so that game would be easier to hunt. Often great fires swept the country as a result. The first settlers used the trees they needed, but there were so many trees that they seemed to be a nuisance.

From the time of settlement in Oregon until 1911, it was estimated that 160 billion board feet of timber went up in smoke. This totaled more than 4 million acres (1.6 million hectares) of the finest trees in the world, and nobody cared. An 1853 newspaper reported that the steamer *Pioneer* was unable to navigate because of smoke from forest fires. As late as 1902 another newspaper account was headlined "Smoke Stops Shipping—Thick Bank Prevents Vessels Reaching Columbia River."

Finally, the people became alarmed at the destruction of their wealth. A state forestry board was set up, and ever since there has been a concerted effort to protect and maintain the forests of Oregon. More than 200,000 acres (80,000 hectares) are reforested each year. Smoke jumpers, who parachute into burning areas to help control back-country fires, are trained in Intercity. The war against damaging insects is carried on.

Insect pests have caused a lot of harm. The European pine shoot moth was brought into the state about 1960, doing great damage to Oregon pines. A shadow of disease has also fallen over the popular Port Orford cedar. When a killing root rot attacks one of these beautiful trees, it cannot be saved.

Oregon's people conserve their timber supply in a variety of ways, including growing trees on tree farms such as this one.

A huge natural disaster occurred in August, 1933, when a fresh east wind swept through the dry forests of Gales Creek. Only one logger was operating in the area. As he pulled in his last log, a spark flew from the equipment. "Flame raced to the top of a tall snag. It broke into flame like a huge candle. The east wind carried burning moss and rotten wood half a mile across the canyon into the slashings." The fire spread like a tornado and burned for ten days; then it seemed to come under control.

But once again "the fire broke out with the violence of a mighty volcano. Great massive thunderheads rolled and surged to a height of 40,000 feet [12,000 meters] and spread out to darken the coastal cities in a weird, unearthly darkness. It rolled through the immense forests of the Coast Range with the howl and roar of a thousand freight trains racing over long trestles. Huge trees were uprooted with the fury of the wind currents. . . . Cities near the Pacific were covered with a mass of ashes, charred twigs and needles. Debris fell on the decks of ships 500 miles [800 kilometers] at sea."

Fog came in that night and helped bring the fire under control, but in only twenty hours 217,000 acres (87,000 hectares) of timber had been destroyed. Altogether this fire, which is known as the Tillamook Burn, destroyed 250,000 acres (100,000 hectares) of timber, a loss of twelve billion board feet.

The timber destroyed in this one disaster was enough to have built a million five-room houses. This was one of the worst forest fires in United States history, and efforts are still being made to restore the area.

In general, however, the forest picture is bright. Oregon's total saw timber has increased at the rate of about five billion board feet per year. That gain could be more than doubled if scientific forest management techniques could be fully utilized throughout the state. Oregon could harvest a great deal more of its timber every year than it does now and still not be in any danger of running out.

By far the largest part of Oregon's forests consists of Douglas fir. The tree is found in thirty-five of the thirty-six counties of Oregon.

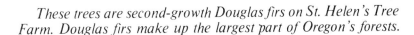

These trees are second-growth Douglas firs on St. Helen's Tree Farm. Douglas firs make up the largest part of Oregon's forests.

The biggest Douglas fir is 15½ feet (5 meters) in diameter; the tallest towered 385 feet (116 meters) into the sky. It may be the tallest tree on record.

Another important tree, number two in Oregon, is the ponderosa pine. The largest stand in the world is growing near Prineville.

The western juniper spreads welcome green over countless miles of dry eastern Oregon, which otherwise would be treeless. This tree is sometimes known as the "camel" of trees, because it can survive on so little water.

Oregon is noted for its beautiful myrtle trees. These grow so evenly shaped that they often appear to have been trimmed. They are found only in southwestern Oregon. Oregon myrtlewood is often compared to the biblical myrtlewood of Palestine, but it is not the same tree.

Oregon boasts three fine groves of redwood trees in Curry County. Other trees include the Port Orford cedar, the wild cherry, with its quinine-like taste, and the Pacific dogwood. The madrone tree sheds its bark as well as its leaves.

A great variety of trees thrives in Oregon, including maples, oaks, Oregon crab apple, willows, poplars, birch, ash, and the golden chinkapin, with its delicious nuts.

A great abundance of plant life may be found in the shadows of the trees or blanketing the meadows or the seashore with bloom. In the relatively small area of Shore Acres State Park, near Coos Bay, there are thirty-five hundred different varieties of trees and plants.

Along the shores bloom silver-tip, seashore lupine, beach snake root, sea rocket, sand verbena, grey beach pea, beach silvertop, Scotch broom, yellow gorse, salmon berry, silk tassel bush, and hundreds more.

The beautiful Camas lily, red-bells, whipple-vine, western azalea, and western peony are among the wild blooms of southwestern Oregon. Eighty-six varieties of plants are found only in this section. One of the weirdest plants of the region is the giant, insect-eating cobra lily, with leaves that form a death trap for insects.

Strawberry Mountain, near Prairie City, takes its name from the abundance of wild strawberries found on its slopes. The slopes of

Mount Hood are noted for colorful heather and brilliant displays of rhododendrons.

ABOUNDING IN THE WATERS

The quantity and variety of fish in Oregon are amazing. One of the world's best-known is Oregon's state fish—the Chinook salmon. It averages fifteen to twenty-five pounds (seven to eleven kilograms), but some weighing almost a hundred pounds (forty-five kilograms) have been caught. The life history of the salmon is known to almost everyone. It leaves its birthplace upstream, makes its way to the ocean, lives most of its life in the sea, finds its way back to its home river, and fights its way back upstream no matter what the obstacles, sometimes a thousand miles (sixteen hundred kilometers), to spawn and die.

Strangely, however, some salmon, such as the kokanee, live all their lives in one place; they are known as landlocked salmon. Just as there are salmon that never go to sea, there are also trout that do go to sea. The steelhead is a kind of seagoing rainbow trout, one of the true migratory fish.

Oregon is one of the great regions for shellfish, as the promoters of Newport point out. On one eighteen-mile (twenty-nine kilometer) stretch of beach, a million razor clams have been harvested in one year. Most people are surprised to know that the natural life of this creature covers a span of five years. Littleneck, horseneck, and cockel are among the other popular clams of Oregon.

Oregon also has crabs and oysters. Deep-sea fishing for sport is said to be at its best in Oregon waters, and a wide variety of commercial fish is taken from the ocean off Oregon.

BEASTS OF THE FIELD AND BIRDS OF THE AIR

Deep in the Sea Lion Caves on the Oregon coast an old sea lion perches on a thronelike rock formation in the center of the main cavern. Here for countless generations, one old chief after another has ruled his herd. This rookery at Sea Lion Point is the only one on the mainland of the United States.

Offshore, at Otter Crescent, is the home of another group, Oregon's famous white sea lions. Here sea turkeys are also found.

Oregon's great variety of natural creatures ranges from the animals of the sea to the mountain goats and bighorn sheep of the Rocky Mountain crags. The call of the Rocky Mountain elk echoes across Oregon's valleys and canyons. Roosevelt elk also roam the countryside. Bear, cougar, wolves, and coyote are all still found in Oregon. A herd of reindeer, imported from Alaska, may be seen at Redmond. Deer of many varieties are the most numerous big game in the state. Mule deer, black-tail deer, white-tail deer, and many others are found.

The pronghorn antelope is renowned for its unusual speed. These animals have been clocked at a continuous thirty miles (forty-eight kilometers) per hour on prolonged runs.

Oregon's State Game Commission gives careful attention to the conservation and protection of these many wild treasures. Hunting is carefully controlled, and the game population thrives; large numbers of hunters can be accommodated. Hunting with bow and arrow is especially popular in Oregon. Eagle Creek Archery Area, opened in 1957, is said to be the best of its kind in the West.

Fur-bearing animals once were the greatest source of wealth in Oregon. Their numbers and their value have long since diminished, but many are still found in the state. The beaver is still important for its water conservation activities. The rare and much-prized sea otter was thought extinct, but a few were found in California and they have increased in numbers.

Small animals abound. Rabbits, skunks, opossum, porcupines, marmot, mountain beaver, and badger all make their home in Oregon.

Oregon's bird population is numerous. Along the shores the tufted puffin, or sea parrot, pigeon guillemot, herring sea gull, cormorant, and sandhill crane are familiar. Upper Klamath Lake is noted for its colony of white pelicans.

Migratory game birds come to Oregon in great numbers on their regular route, the Pacific flyway. Although many of these fly beyond Oregon to winter, some flocks make their winter home in the state and breed there. These include many varieties of duck and geese.

Another popular game bird in Oregon is the pheasant. Lovers of the pheasant all over the United States have a particular reason to thank Oregon. The first pheasants in the United States were brought into Linn County from China in 1882. After that small beginning, the pheasant population in the United States spread throughout the country.

The Tule Lake National Wildlife Refuge, shown here in a painting by John W. McCoy, is famous as the site of the largest annual concentration of waterfowl on the North American continent.

Much of Oregon has an abundance of water. Colville Indians caught enough salmon in two months at Kettle Falls on the Columbia River to feed them all year. 1847 painting by Canadian artist Paul Kane.

PARADISE FOR ROCK HOUNDS

Oregon has been called the Agate State. Probably no other similar area possesses such a quantity and variety of agates. Rock hounds, people who make a pastime of gathering beautiful stones, shuffle along the beaches searching for rare and beautiful agates. Agate Beach has long been noted for its profusion of these beautiful stones. The rare saginite agate has been found on beaches. Agates are also found at many places in the interior. The city of Prineville owns twenty-five claims where rock hounds may dig free.

Ribbon agate, holley blue, moss, carnelian, water, tiger eye, and many other kinds of agates may be found. In many localities agate shops will cut and polish the visitor's agate finds, or even mount them in jewelry.

Many other semiprecious stones are found in Oregon. Near Prineville are the largest deposits of jasper, chalcedony, and quartz in Oregon. Obsidian and petrified wood are found near Burns, as well as in other parts of the state. Oregon jade, although not of great commercial value, is prized by many a discoverer.

54

Much of Oregon's mineral wealth remains untapped commercially, but the state is a land of almost unlimited potential in minerals. Reserves of 23,000,000 short tons (20,865,000 metric tons) of nickel are known.

Bauxite, source of aluminum, is known to exist in Oregon to the extent of 100,000,000 short tons (90,718,500 metric tons). Building stone, insulating materials, clays, perlite, quartz, salt brines, glass sand, and other valuable minerals are found extensively. Fifty million tons (45,360,000 metric tons) of bituminous coal and a billion tons (907,185,000 metric tons) of sub-bituminous coal are estimated in the state's reserves.

HOT AND COLD RUNNING WATER

One of the first natural resources ever used by human beings was fresh water. Water for drinking, bathing, kitchen, and commercial use is still one of the world's most valuable treasures.

Although large portions of Oregon have little water, much of the state has an abundance.

At its mouth, the Columbia River runs with the second-greatest volume of water and the most powerful flow of all the rivers within the country.

The Coast and Cascade ranges catch large amounts of rain and huge snowfalls, providing tremendous runoffs of mountain water. This water is so pure that in many cases it can be used in chemical and industrial processes without any purification.

In addition to surface water supplies, large amounts of ground water are found in many localities.

Waters heated below the surface of the earth find many outlets in Oregon. A natural storehouse of steam below Klamath Falls melts the snow on the street and is used to heat houses. Mineral springs abound in the state. At Ashland, Lithia-mineral spring water is piped for various uses, and it gushes from the fountain in the plaza. Kitson Hot Mineral Springs near Oakridge is said to be one of the finest in the United States.

The Weyerhaeuser Company turns timber into plywood.

People Use Their Treasures

TEN BILLION BOARD FEET

How do you use ten billion board feet of wood a year? That is no problem to the American people. Oregon has led the nation in lumber production since 1939. The timber cut every year in Oregon ends up in a huge variety of products.

The most valuable and useful of all Oregon lumber comes from the Douglas fir. More products come from this tree than from any other kind.

One of the most useful materials of modern-day living—commercial plywood—originated in Oregon. Today the state produces more than 67 percent of all the nation's plywood. The world's largest Douglas fir plywood plant is located at Lebanon.

A large percent of all the country's hardboard, chipboard, and insulation board comes from Oregon. Wood shingles and shakes, wood pulp, paper and paper board, Christmas trees and greens pour from Oregon's rich forests in an unending stream.

Each year discoveries of new uses for wood add value to every board foot cut in Oregon. Still, millions of tons of wood materials now go to waste annually. This includes slabs, trims, edgings, sawdust, shavings, cores, and bark. As new industries come to the state and new uses are found, it is expected that much of such waste will go into useful products.

In addition to the giant forest industries, Oregon has many small and interesting activities based on its tree products.

Cone picking adds to the income of many college students and other part-time workers. During a good cone year, hundreds of pickers earn money harvesting cones from the tops of swaying trees. These cones provide seeds for use in reforesting.

Some of Oregon's specialty woods are famous. Port Orford cedar is an unusual wood, especially prized for boat building. Oregon myrtlewood, known throughout the world for its beautiful grain, is used by many manufacturers to create a wide variety of wooden novelties, such as trays, candleholders, and jewelry boxes.

OLD McLOUGHLIN HAD A FARM

Next to lumbering, agriculture is the largest industry of Oregon. Every year income of more than a billion dollars is realized from the state's agriculture. Willamette Valley is one of the most productive agricultural areas of the world.

Oregon leads the country in the production of winter pears, snap beans, and filberts. In fact, most of America's filberts come from Oregon. The state ranks second in strawberries, sweet cherries, plums, prunes, and walnuts, and third in green peas. Oregon has nationwide leadership in one unusual crop—turf and forage grass seed, including Merion bluegrass, bent grass, rye grass, alsike clover, and fescue. The lawns and golf courses of the country look to Imbler for their seed, while 82 percent of the nation's bent grass is grown in the Stayton area.

Wheat and hay are the state's largest crops in dollar volume, with vegetables next. Potatoes, sugar beets, onions, cabbage, corn, and other standard crops thrive in many parts of the state. Milton-Freewater has been called the Pea Capital of the World.

Old Dr. John McLoughlin was the first to prove that crops and fruit could be grown in the Oregon region. However, fruit growing first became an industry in Oregon when Henderson Luelling brought in trees to Milwaukie from Iowa. Today, Hood River is the center of the state's fruit-growing region. Medford is a name that means "pears" throughout most of the United States. At least five varieties of pears are grown there.

Livestock, dairying, poultry, and eggs bring more millions to the pockets of Oregon farmers. Millions of cattle and sheep fatten on the ranges of the state. One of the country's greatest turkey centers is at McMinnville.

Oregon is a leader in nursery and horticultural materials. It is first in the production of Easter lily bulbs; when huge fields of these lilies are in bloom, the countryside seems to be one huge flower garden. Another flower crop, the stately dahlia, provides a spectacular show of blooms in Clackamas County, where the Swan Island Dahlia Farms are the largest producers of dahlias in the Western

Vast and fertile fields make agriculture Oregon's second largest industry.

Hemisphere. Other flowering bulbs, perennials, shrubs, and trees for landscaping add to Oregon's predominance in commercial plants. The state is also first in holly production.

WHEN IS NICKEL WORTH MORE THAN GOLD?

In 1851 two mule drivers named Boole and Cluggage were grazing their animals in the Jacksonville region when they made that most exciting of all discoveries—gold! A typical mining boom began. The bank of C.C. Beekman at Jacksonville welcomed thirty-one million dollars' worth of gold over its counters during the twenty-seven years of the gold period in that area. Today the old bank is closed, but it may be seen just as the Beekman family left it, with the scales still ready to weigh gold dust and nuggets.

At Gold Beach, mining was profitable until the floods of 1861 washed the sands away. Eastern Oregon also had its gold rush. In 1862, the biggest year of the Burnt Powder River and John Day River gold regions, twenty million dollars' worth of the gleaming metal was taken.

Today, although some gold is still found in Oregon, nickel production brings far more revenue to Oregon. Oregon is the only state with a producing nickel mine in the United States. It is also one of only five states now producing mercury ores.

Clays, building stones, sand, gravel, and other nonmetallic minerals have by far the largest dollar value of all of Oregon's mineral industry.

Albany, Oregon, has become a world center in the highly specialized, and often secret, field of reactive metals such as hafnium, zirconium, and titanium. Processes for purifying and reducing these metals were discovered in the Northwest Regional Development Laboratories of the United States Bureau of Mines at Albany, Oregon. The know-how stayed at Albany. Three Albany companies entered the reactive metals field—Oregon Metallurgical Corporation, Wah Chang Corporation, and Northwest Industries, Inc. These firms and Development Laboratories have made Albany the nation's reactive metals research and production center.

Zirconium and titanium sponge and ingots are produced, and titanium products are manufactured—all highly technical processes. Research continues to develop and apply such rare metals as columbium and tantalum.

MANY DAM SITES

Forty percent of all the nation's water-power potential is found in the Columbia River and its tributaries. Much of this powerful water flows by or through Oregon. Today, the state is third in the nation in hydroelectric development. However, only little less than a fourth of the possible water power in Oregon is being used. Even now Oregon uses the largest amount of electric power per family in the nation.

John Day Dam on the Columbia, just below the mouth of the John Day River, ranks second in the country in capacity to produce electric power. Besides providing power, Oregon's great dams give protection from floods and runoffs, provide water for irrigation, and often improve navigation. The John Day Dam overcomes numerous rapids, such as Squalley Hook and Indian. Bonneville, the Dalles, and McNary dams all help to control the Columbia.

The Snake River already is controlled by Oxbow, Brownlee, and Hell's Canyon dams. Owyhee Dam and Owyhee Lake on the Owyhee River bring a great reserve of water to a dry area.

When all the dams are completed on the Willamette River and its tributaries, it will be one of the most completely regulated of all major rivers. Hills Creek, Dexter, Fern Ridge, Cottage Grove, Dorena, and Detroit are some of the dams in this region.

When all the dams are completed on the Willamette River, shown below, it will be one of the most completely regulated of all major rivers.

FUR AND FIN

In early days, the great quantities of salmon in Oregon's coastal rivers provided food for the Indians, and in many regions their whole economy was based on the salmon. Sometimes as many as a thousand Indians might be seen fishing at a single location. They dried salmon into a food called pemmican. It remained edible for years and could be used to trade for goods the Indians needed from other tribes.

In the 1860s a new process of preserving salmon in tin cans was used on the Columbia. By 1883 nearly forty canneries were packing salmon. Astoria had become the center of the industry. There was so much waste that bears "bumming a meal" became a problem. Seals were also a problem; the canners employed a full-time sharpshooter to pick off raiding seals.

A large colony of Chinese came in as cannery workers. Experienced Scandinavian fisherman also headed for the Oregon country in large numbers. So many Finns settled in the Astoria area that it has been called Finland in America.

For a time it looked as if sturgeon might become a commercial fish in Oregon. Some sturgeon "farmers" went so far as to fence off small bays for holding captured sturgeon until they had grown large enough for market. One sturgeon reached 1,800 pounds (810 kilograms). However, the number of sturgeon decreased until the great fish had to be carefully protected.

One commercial fishing operation provides fish food for mink farms. Today such farms raise more fur animals in captivity than are trapped. Although the fur trade was the first commercial enterprise in Oregon, and at one time 175 ships operated in the fur trade, trapping now brings in only a small income.

MANUFACTURING

The greatest volume of manufacturing in Oregon at the present time has to do with the processing of forest products. The next-largest industry is the processing and preserving of food products. More than forty different agricultural crops are processed. Salem is considered the second-largest fruit and vegetable processing center in the United States.

Oregon is noted for its dairy industry, especially Tillamook cheese. One cheese company in Tillamook County operates the largest cheese factory in the world.

Metal fabrication is another major industry.

The electronics industry has become strongly established in the Portland metropolitan area.

Industry in Oregon is growing rapidly in variety and type. Everything from church furniture to dry ice is produced in Oregon. Jams and syrups, organs, adhesives, trailers, snow vehicles, knitted wear, paper, cake flour, beer, and batteries all add to the outpouring of products worth about $4½ billion every year.

TRANSPORTATION AND COMMUNICATION

Modern highways have replaced the ruts of the Oregon Trail. Jet planes zoom over the wildernesses in minutes. Once the dash of pony express riders across the 225-mile (360-kilometer) stretch between the Dalles and Canyon City was the most efficient means of communication. Now the people in those communities, and elsewhere in Oregon, can watch television in their living rooms and view events halfway across the world the instant they take place.

Some up-to-date transportation came to Oregon early in its history. Steamboats were in regular operation on the Columbia by 1850. By 1853 fourteen river steamers were calling regularly at Portland. This port sent out its first full shipload of wheat in 1868 and is now the major export center for western wheat to the Orient. Located 101 miles (162 kilometers) inland, Portland is the only deep freshwater port on the Pacific. About sixty-five steamship lines operate out of this inland city.

Another notable Oregon port is Coos Bay, known as the World's Largest Lumber Shipping Port.

Before the advent of modern transportation, stagecoaches carried both passengers and mail. Here the California-Oregon stage is shown as it passes Mount Shasta.

Railroads came more slowly to this remote land, with its difficult terrain. The first railroad steam engine in Oregon hauled freight for ten miles (sixteen kilometers) around Celilo Falls. This historic little engine, known as the Pony, is now on display at Portland.

When it was proposed that southern Oregon be connected with California by rail, some unhappy residents said that only two trains would ever be needed—one to take away all the discontented Oregon residents, and the other to come along and pick up the tracks.

Despite doubt and difficulties, rail development progressed. When two rival railroads competed for the rights to a particularly rich area, there was often great excitement. James J. Hill of the Great Northern Railroad and E.H. Harriman of the Union Pacific often fought for rights in Oregon.

When railroads would not come to them, some Oregon communities built their own. The nineteen-mile (thirty-kilometer) Prineville Railroad was built and operated by Prineville to provide a connection with the Union Pacific mainline.

Oregon's first newspaper was the *Spectator* of Oregon City. Established in 1846, it is claimed to be the first newspaper published in the entire Northwest. Today, the *Oregonian* and *Oregon Journal,* both of Portland, are the state's largest newspapers.

Human Treasures

THE FATHER OF OREGON

One of the most remarkable men in the history of the North American continent has been called the Father of Oregon. Dr. John McLoughlin became a legend while he lived.

His appearance was so striking that many of the Indians almost worshipped him. He towered more than six feet (two meters) in height, and his snow-white hair hung to his shoulders. It had turned white by the time he was forty.

John McLoughlin was born in Canada in 1784 and trained as a doctor. He entered the service of the Hudson's Bay Company and rose rapidly with the company. He helped to arrange the union of the Canadian Northwest and Hudson's Bay companies. Then he became the chief factor of the newly formed company, the second most powerful company position in all of North America.

When he became governor of the company's operations in the American West, he exercised so much power and authority that he was called "the only feudal lord in the history of the North American continent."

But it was not his executive genius that made him so well liked in Oregon; it was his kindness to the settlers.

Author Eva Dye tells about the coming of the immigrants of 1844: "Again winter rains were beating up the Cascades. Already December snows were whirling around Mt. Hood. Snowbound cattle were famishing on the mountain trails, weary mothers were dragging their children along the slippery portages. Emaciated, discouraged, exhausted, the silent tears dropped down their hollow cheeks as they thought of the comfortable homes they had left in the States; but as a rule the women were brave, braver than the men. The dogs were killed and eaten, the last spare garment was traded for a sack of potatoes. Wet to the skin, shivering around their green campfires while the damp flakes fell, they even envied the comfort of the Indians lying flat on the clean sand under the huge projecting rocks, secure from the storm.

"Dr. McLoughlin sent a relief expedition. His agent said, 'Dr. McLoughlin was afraid you might be in trouble. He has sent a bateau of provisions, also some clothing.'

" 'But—' hesitated one, thankful, yet abashed.

" 'Do not apologize, sir,' said the agent kindly; 'take what you need. Those who can pay may do so. Those who cannot must not be left to suffer. Such are the doctor's orders. Boats are on the way to help you down to Fort Vancouver.' "

When they reached the fort the doctor offered to furnish the provisions they needed to get started in Oregon. " 'But, sir,' broke in several, 'we have no money.'

" 'Tut, tut, tut! Never mind that. You can't suffer,' said the doctor. Glancing at the head man, — 'Sir, your name, if you please. How many in the family? What do you desire?' and so of each the questions were asked and orders made out.

" 'Here, gentlemen, take these to the clerks; they will supply your immediate needs. The rest you can obtain later. All can be paid at our house in Oregon City when your crops come in.'

"Profoundly moved, one by one they bowed themselves out from the presence of that 'old barbarian in his den on the Columbia,' as some had previously called him, whose generosity had rescued them and their families from suffering, starvation, and possibly death. . . .

"In Bachelors' Hall the lads indited the first letters since leaving St. Joe in May. . . . Scarcely had they finished when a servant entered with roast beef and potatoes, and the boys dined like guests in the home of a friend. . . . Dr. McLoughlin so bestowed favors that the recipient felt honored by the contact."

As more and more settlers came in, Dr. McLoughlin's hold on the Oregon country became less secure. The men of his Hudson's Bay Company could see their influence, and their profits, declining. They blamed Dr. McLoughlin. When they asked him to report, the doctor wrote: "Gentlemen, as a man of common humanity I could not do otherwise than to give those naked and starving people to eat and to wear of our stores. I foresaw clearly that it aided the American settlement of the country, but this I cannot help. It is not for me, but for God, to look after and take care of the consequences."

The John McLoughlin House in Oregon City,
Clackamas County, is now a national shrine.

So the "emperor" of the Oregon Territory resigned his position, built a house on his property at Oregon City, and settled down to become an American. While most of his neighbors honored and respected him, a few envied and disliked him. Congress approved all claims of settlers to Oregon land except those of Dr. McLoughlin. This stripped him of practically all his property.

He had renounced his British citizenship; when the United States refused to grant him citizenship, the once all-powerful ruler of Oregon became a man without a country, tired, ill, and old.

Five years after McLoughlin died, the Oregon state legislature restored his property to his heirs. In 1921 Dr. John McLoughlin was chosen to be one of the two men to represent Oregon in the National Hall of Fame in the Capitol at Washington. His house is a national shrine.

JASON LEE

High on the list of the pioneers of Oregon would be the name of the Reverend Jason Lee. In one of the finest locations of the Willamette Valley, the Lees built a log mission, twenty by thirty feet (six by ten meters), "with chimney of sticks and clay. Jason Lee had swung the broadaxe that hewed the logs; Daniel Lee had calked the crevices with moss. There were Indian mats on the hewn-fir floors, home-made stools and tables. The hearth was of baked clay and ashes, the batten doors hung on leather hinges and clicked with wooden latches. Four small windows let in the light through squares of dried deerskin set in sashes carved by the jack-knife of Jason Lee."

At this mission they preached and taught. The white settlers were mostly French Canadians, formerly employed by the Hudson's Bay Company. Although they were Catholics, they listened to the preaching of the Lees. Most of these men had married Indian women, and their children were taught in the Lees' school.

Jason Lee was a bachelor. He sent word to his mission headquarters in the East that he would like to have a young lady come West who might consent to be his bride. With other missionaries, Anna Maria Pitman made the long trip by boat around Cape Horn and arrived at Fort Vancouver, where Jason Lee came to meet her. They returned to the mission by canoe, where they were met by Governor McLoughlin.

The two were married by Daniel Lee in the first Anglo-Saxon wedding ceremony on the Pacific Coast.

Disappointments stalked Jason Lee's later life. The death of Anna Maria, and then of a second wife, saddened him. He was removed from his post as the head of the mission. He died in the East while trying to raise funds for an Oregon university.

In spite of the disregard he received in later life, Jason Lee is recognized as the founder of Oregon's capital city of Salem, and of Willamette University.

SOME OTHER PIONEERS

Ewing Young was one of the leading men in the fur trade, with headquarters at Taos, New Mexico. A young man named Kit Carson got his early training on the frontier from Young. When Young came to Oregon, he had a difficult time. Dr. McLoughlin thought he was a horse thief and refused to give him a stake. However, when Young decided to go to California to buy cattle, even Dr. McLoughlin invested five hundred dollars. The settlers desperately needed cattle. Altogether they raised fifteen hundred dollars, and Young sailed with his men to California. There he bought six hundred cattle. The journey back overland was a difficult one, spent fighting off the Indians, scaling the mountains, and racing the coming winter. But Young and his men made it back. The settlers, as one account puts it, "had won a race against starvation and death. It was a race, literally, for freedom."

Dr. McLoughlin was on hand to shake Young's hand and congratulate him, although this was one of the turning points against the hold of the Hudson's Bay Company in Oregon.

When Young died, he was one of the richest men in the region. He left no will, and there was no government in the country to dispose of his estate. When the settlers gathered to elect officers to administer Young's property, they laid the basis for the provisional government of Oregon.

Joe Gale had been one of the drivers in Ewing Young's cattle drive. When he and some of the other men of the Willamette Valley began to build a ship, few ever thought they would succeed. They laid the keel on Swan Island. All the beams, planks, and wooden parts had to be cut by hand. Every nail had to be made by hand. Dr.

McLoughlin refused to sell them the hardware and rigging they needed, because their credit had run out. But a United States ship came to Fort Vancouver, and the commander persuaded McLoughlin to change his mind. Joe Gale and four helpers stuck to it. By June, 1842, the very first ship ever made in Oregon was ready to sail. Joe Gale called it the *Star of Oregon* and sailed it to Fort Vancouver, with the stars and stripes on the mast.

Joe and the other four builders sailed their pioneer craft down the coast to California. There they sold it for 350 cattle. Joe also persuaded forty American families in California to move north to Oregon. Altogether twelve hundred cattle, three thousand sheep, and several hundred horses and mules were driven up the trail blazed by Ewing Young to the Willamette Valley. This left the valley forever independent of the Hudson's Bay Company.

PRINCES OF COPPER SKIN

The Nez Percé tribe was widely admired by whites in the United States. The names of their two greatest chiefs, Old Joseph and Young Joseph, are still among the best remembered in the Oregon country.

Young Chief Joseph tried every legal means for twenty years to regain his tribe's lost rights in the beautiful Wallowa Valley. The Nez Percé went to war with the whites only in desperation; it was a war of defense and not offense.

At the close of their heroic retreat, Chief Joseph made a sad speech. "I am tired of fighting. My people ask me for food, and I have none to give. It is cold, and we have no blankets, no wood. My people are starving to death. Where is my little daughter? I do not know. Perhaps, even now, she is freezing to death. Hear me, my chiefs, I have fought; but from where the sun now stands, Joseph will fight no more." He walked slowly toward the American camp, with his blanket hiding his face, to surrender.

Today, Oregon's Indian citizens are among the country's leaders, upholding the dignity of the Indian people and bringing them honor.

CREATIVE SPIRITS

One of the great leaders in natural science was David Douglas, who came to the Oregon country in 1825 and spent two years there, exploring, studying, and obtaining samples of its trees and plants. He returned in 1830. Douglas suffered many of the hardships of the pioneers. His name is remembered in the Douglas fir tree, the Douglas maple, and in Douglas County, Oregon.

Another naturalist, John Muir, spent only a short time in Oregon, but his writings about the country have become important. He wrote, "Who could ever guess that so rough a wilderness should yet be so fine, so full of good things. One seems to be in a majestic, domed pavilion in which a grand play is being acted with scenery and music and incense."

In literature, Edwin Markham, author of *The Man with the Hoe,* was born in Oregon City. Author Frederic Homer Balch, born near Albany, Oregon, wrote a best seller based on a legend about a great natural stone bridge that once actually may have spanned the Columbia. He called his book *The Bridge of the Gods,* and it went through twenty-nine printings.

Oregonians include such artists as sculptor Ralph Stackpole and prominent cartoonist Homer Davenport. The classical composer Ernest Bloch wrote some of his best-known works in his rambling home on the bluff overlooking Agate Beach. Stewart Holbrook made his home in Portland for many years and achieved fame as an author and historian.

Teaching and Learning

The first school in Oregon was taught by Solomon H. Smith at Wheatland in 1834. The first free public schools were established in Oregon only twelve years later, in 1845. This is something of a record. Many of the very old states to the east did not have free public schools until later.

The Reverend Jason Lee's school at Salem became the Oregon Institute and finally Willamette University, the oldest institution of higher learning in the West.

First of the state-owned colleges was Oregon State College at Corvallis, founded in 1868 as one of the land-grant colleges. It was a continuation of Corvallis College, which began in 1852 as a Methodist school. Today called Oregon State University, it is the second largest higher-education institute in the state.

The University of Oregon was opened in 1876 at Eugene. A group of residents of Eugene had pledged fifty thousand dollars toward a university there. One of the contributions was a fat hog. In a relatively short period the university has grown to become a leading institution. Its museum's collection of rare Oriental art is especially noteworthy. Among its campuses outside Eugene are the College of Medicine and Dentistry at Portland, and the Institute of Marine Biology at Charleston.

Eastern Oregon State College at La Grande is the only four-year college in Oregon east of the Cascades. Old College Hall of Pacific University, Forest Grove, is said to be the oldest building west of the Mississippi still used for higher education.

Some other Oregon colleges and universities include the University of Portland, Reed College, and Lewis and Clark College, all of Portland; Southern Oregon State College, Ashland; Pacific University, Forest Grove; Linfield College, McMinnville; Oregon College of Education, Monmouth; and Oregon Institute of Technology, Klamath Falls.

Opposite: Deady Hall, the first building on the University of Oregon campus, is now on the National Register of Historic Buildings.

Enchantment of Oregon

INCOMPARABLE COAST

Oregon's scenic coast stretches 296 miles (476 kilometers). Only a few miles are in private hands. All the rest of Oregon's beaches are in the public domain, preserved for such recreations as clamming, boating, surfing, and especially beachcombing. A touch of the Orient may be found by the beachcomber who picks up one of the many Japanese glass fishing floats that have drifted over the Pacific from Japan.

Highway 101 follows the old Indian trail along the coast. The traveler who begins his tour at historic Astoria finds himself in the oldest American city in the West. Astor Column is a unique memorial, with a spiral frieze circling from bottom to top, 125 feet (38 meters) above the ground, picturing the history of the area.

Nearby Fort Stevens for years was the only coastal fortification in Oregon. It has been restored and is now part of a state park. The wreck of the *Peter Iredale* (it sank in 1906) is a grim scenic attraction of the area.

Fort Clatsop, built by Lewis and Clark as their winter headquarters, was entirely reconstructed as Fort Clatsop National Memorial.

Seaside is the oldest seashore town in Oregon. Its concrete promenade stretches for two miles (three kilometers) along the shore and is the longest of its kind. At Seaside, a monument commemorates Lewis and Clark.

More than two hundred years ago a Spanish galleon was wrecked on the shore near Manzanita. Its cargo of beeswax was spilled out, and even today lumps of the beeswax are still being found. Also near Manzanita, Neah-Kah-Nie Mountain Viewpoint provides a magnificent view from a height of 1,700 feet (510 meters) above the surf.

In 1846 the U.S. schooner *Shark* was washed ashore. A cannon from the ship was found near where the wreck occurred, and ever

Opposite: Herita Head Lighthouse on the Oregon Coast.

Arch Rock at Rockaway is only one of the many strange rock formations to be found on the Oregon Coast.

since the spot has been called Cannon Beach. Nearby "Haystack," jutting 300 feet (90 meters) out of the Pacific Ocean, is one of the largest rocks on the coast.

Near Tillamook is Cape Lookout State Park.

Devil's Lake is a popular boating spot, and many racing records have been set there. Inland is the town of Grande Ronde.

The coast north of Newport has been described as one of the most spectacular in the world. The viewpoint at Beverly State Park is heavily photographed. White sea lions, Oregon pelicans, and sea turkeys add to the interest of the scene. At the Lookout is a fine collection of driftwood and Japanese floats. Nearby Agate Beach is one of the world's finest hunting grounds for agate collectors.

At Newport, Highway 20 comes to a halt at the Pacific Ocean, after crossing the continent from Boston, Massachusetts.

One of the outstanding attractions of the coast is Sea Lion Caves. Visitors never tire of watching the sea lions—the old bulls jealously guarding their harems, and the playful pups cavorting. One of the natural rock formations within the cave is said to resemble a sculpture of Lincoln.

76

North Bend is the largest city on the south Oregon Coast. Nearby Coquille is noted for the factories that make articles from native myrtlewood. Battle Rock, near Port Orford, commemorates the pioneers who fought off the Indians there.

Oregon's Rogue River is spectacular. One of the most famous sightseeing trips in the country is the 64-mile (102-kilometer) round-trip passenger ride on the mail boats. Sometimes the ranch dogs come down to the dock to pick up the mail and carry it back to their masters.

Brookings is probably the only community anywhere with two state parks within its city limits—Harris and Azalea. Azalea State Park abounds in colorful azaleas, some of them wild plants hundreds of years old. Brookings holds an annual Azalea Festival each May. In the fields around Brookings are grown 75 percent of all American Easter lilies.

Azalea State Park (below) is one of two state parks in Brookings.

SOUTHWESTERN OREGON

Over the mountains from the southern coast are a number of picturesque communities, including Jacksonville. The town grew up after gold was discovered in 1852. It was surveyed using a chicken coop as the principal marker. When the chicken coop disintegrated, most of the town's property titles were in doubt. The Oddfellows' building, still standing in Jacksonville, was constructed with 2 feet (.6 meter) of dirt between the roof and ceiling to protect it from Indian fire arrows.

Legend says that the Jacksonville Methodist Church was built from the contribution of one night's take at the community's gambling tables. Another legend says that when the varnish on the pews of the Presbyterian church failed to dry, the pews were decorated with bustles and trouser seats. Much of the pioneer tradition of the area has been preserved in Jacksonville's Museum of History.

Ashland has an international reputation in the arts. In 1935 A.L. Bowmer founded a Shakespeare festival there. America's first Elizabethan theater was built, and this remote corner of Oregon became renowned for its fine presentation of Shakespeare's plays.

Ashland's Lithia Park was designed by John McLaren, who went on to lay out Golden Gate Park in San Francisco. Ashland is also the site of the Southern Oregon Museum of Natural Resources.

Near the Oregon-California border, Oregon Caves, now a national monument, are almost as spectacular as Carlsbad Caverns. The Oregon Caves were discovered by Elijah Davidson in 1874. Poet Joaquin Miller called them the Marble Halls of Oregon and did a great deal to promote interest in them.

To the east is Klamath Falls, where Oregon Institute of Technology is located. The logging museum near Klamath Falls is the largest museum of lumbering in the nation.

Klamath Falls is the closest major town to Crater Lake. The story is told that Paul Bunyan came out of his house one day and found that a tremendous amount of snow had fallen. This was no ordinary snow. It was bright blue. Paul was afraid it might discolor his property, so he looked around for a place to put it. He found the crater

78

Crater Lake (above) is one of the bluest lakes in the world.

of an old volcano and shoveled the blue snow into it. When the snow melted, it formed one of the bluest lakes in the world.

In actual fact, John Wesley Hillman was the first non-Indian to view Crater Lake. It is easy to imagine his amazement when he came to the top of what is now Discovery Point on June 12, 1853. One of the glories of Crater Lake is the fact that it can be viewed as a whole from such points as the Watchman, 1,800 feet (540 meters) above the water. From this point, also, on a clear day the sweep of scenery is so vast that Mount Shasta looms on the far horizon, 100 miles (160 kilometers) away.

Judge William Gladstone Steel devoted fifteen years to a campaign to preserve this natural wonder as a national park. His dream became law on May 22, 1902.

International Rose Test Gardens (above) help maintain Portland's reputation as the City of Roses. Below: A ship in Portland Harbor.

Today the visitor can view the lake from every angle. A thirty-five mile (fifty-six kilometer) road circles it entirely. The lake is said to be at its bluest in the winter. From Rim Village a trail leads to the lake shore.

To the north of Crater Lake towers Mount Thielsen, shaped very much like the European Matterhorn.

THE BLOOM IS ON THE ROSE: PORTLAND

In 1842 Francis W. Pettygrove and Amos Lovejoy founded a town on the Willamette River. It was not a very impressive project. Lovejoy wanted to name the new town in honor of Boston, while Pettygrove suggested naming it Portland for his home town in Maine. They tossed a coin, and Pettygrove won.

Some called the place "Stump Town," because the stumps of trees had not yet been removed from Portland's streets, although they had been whitewashed to make them show up better at night.

Portland grew quickly. Deepwater ships could stop at its docks. Farmers of the Willamette Valley could reach it easily to sell their produce and buy goods. By 1851 the city was incorporated.

Farmers still bring their goods to Portland; it is the leading grain terminal west of the Mississippi and ranks second only to Boston as a wool-marketing center. It is also one of the leading convention centers of the West, with three large auditoriums, including the Memorial Coliseum. Its Lloyd shopping center covers thirty-six square blocks on the east side.

Portland's reputation as the City of Roses is well deserved. The flowers grow everywhere. The rose festival is one of the city's annual celebrations. The first annual rose show opened in 1889, but the rose festival parade began in 1907 with flower-bedecked and illuminated trolley cars. A year later, the Rose Festival Association was formed. Now the festivities last for ten days.

One of the most beautiful rose centers in the City of Roses is International Rose Test Gardens, with its famous statue of Sacajawea, the Indian woman who guided Lewis and Clark. Another famous garden is Lambert. The American Rhododendron Society Test Garden features thirty-five hundred rhododendron plants, blooming in a setting of towering fir trees. Hoyt Arboretum has the nation's largest collection of trees with needle foliage.

For a city of its size, the museums and zoo of Portland are remarkable. The Oregon Building, left over from the Lewis and Clark Exposition of 1905, used to be known as the largest log cabin in the world. The interior was dominated by fifty-two enormous log support pillars. Unfortunately, it was completely destroyed by fire on August 17, 1964. The Oregon Museum of Science and Industry and Planetarium are among the finest of their type. The planetarium is the only one in the Northwest. The Portland Art Museum houses the Rassmussen collection, one of the world's finest collections of Indian art and artifacts. The Museum of the Oregon Historical Society has a collection of mementos of Captain Robert Gray and of Lewis and Clark.

The Portland Zoo has an international reputation. Belle, the zoo's famous mother elephant, was featured in newspaper headlines around the world when her baby was born. The zoo houses the largest colony of Antarctic penguins in captivity.

Portland's Junior Symphony Orchestra has an unusual program which engages famous composers to write symphonic works especially for young people.

Portland is the only United States mainland city with two extinct volcanoes—Mount Tabor and Rocky Butte.

THE MOUNTAIN OF MY LORD HOOD

One of the glories of the Portland "skyline" is another extinct volcanic cone—the snowcapped crest of Mount Hood.

The top of Mount Hood was reached for the first time in 1857. In 1859, and again in 1868, volcanic activities were noted on the mountain. Fumes and gases still come from some of its vents.

There is a story about the origin of Mount Hood. Paul Bunyan built an enormous campfire; when it was time for him to move on,

Mount Hood makes a beautiful backdrop for the Portland skyline.

he tried to put the fire out but had little success. Finally, he piled rocks on the fire. It took so many rocks that he created Mount Hood.

Timberline Lodge on Mount Hood, constructed by the W.P.A. during the Depression, looks as if it might have been built by Paul Bunyan. Every piece of furniture, the striking fabrics, and metalcraft accessories were hand-made of native mineral. It is further decorated by wood carvings and sketches made by W.P.A. artists. The lodge was dedicated by President Franklin D. Roosevelt in 1937. During the winter, when skiing is at its height, the lodge seems dwarfed by the mountains of snow that fall there. The Ski Bus to Timberline Lodge is one of the most unusual cable-car rides anywhere; the cars are actually as large as buses.

The beauty of the region is preserved in Mount Hood National Forest, and hardy climbers now may take any one of nine different routes to its summit.

83

THE VALLEY

Winding past Mount Hood is another hiking route—Skyline Trail—following the crest of the Cascades almost entirely across the state. Hikers on this trail get many unusual glimpses of Oregon's great treasure—the rich valley of the Willamette River.

In that valley, at the place where the Willamette falls forty feet (twelve meters), there was an ancient Indian village. Every year large groups of Indians gathered there to spear the homing salmon. There, beginning in 1825, white people also built a village and called it Oregon City, the first city west of the Rockies to be incorporated. As with so many beginnings in Oregon, Dr. John McLoughlin was responsible for founding Oregon City. There McLoughlin built his house, and there he died. Today, that house has become a national historic site. Another of the Hudson's Bay Company pioneers buried at Oregon City is Peter Skene Ogden.

The Methodist church at Oregon City is claimed to have been the first Protestant church west of the Rockies. Unfortunately, the first public building in Oregon City was the jail. The city is built on two levels, separated by basalt cliffs. To permit people to move freely from one level to another, the city has installed free public elevator service.

In 1812 the first European dwelling and trading post was established in the Willamette Valley. To this spot later came the Reverend Lee, and there the town of Salem developed. In 1852, after great controversy, Salem was named the capital by vote of the people.

The present capitol building is one of the country's most modern state capitols. Fire destroyed the previous building in 1935, and the present building was begun in 1936. Two years later the structure was dedicated.

Oregon's capitol is made of snowy white marble, its round tower topped by a huge statue weighing eight and a half tons, covered with shining gold leaf. This statue represents the Oregon Pioneer. The capitol building itself was a pioneer in the use of pierced-stone window decorations. The colorful and dramatic murals inside show various scenes of Oregon history, including Captain Gray's discovery of the Columbia, Lewis and Clark at Celilo Falls, Dr. McLoughlin meeting the first white women pioneers, the migration of 1843, and the Champoeg meeting. Some of the murals have been reproduced in this book. A massive table in the governor's reception room is made of Carpathian elm, inlaid with a picture of the former capitol, made of forty different kinds of wood.

Outside, the north entrance to the capitol is flanked by two magnificent white marble statues, one showing Lewis and Clark being guided by Sacajawea, and the other a pioneer family on the Oregon Trail. Statues of Jason Lee and Dr. McLoughlin also brighten the grounds.

Willamette University at Salem, oldest in the West, founded by Jason Lee, has an outstanding law school. Salem Art Museum at

The modern white marble state capitol building in Salem.

Bush House, the Oregon State Fair, and the dramatic Marion County Court House are all of interest to the Salem visitor.

East of Salem is Silver Falls State Park, with the largest concentration of waterfalls found anywhere in an area of this size. This is Oregon's largest state park, 8,000 acres (3,200 hectares) in area.

Many of the smaller towns of the Willamette Valley are historic. Newberg was the first Quaker settlement west of the Rocky Mountains. Here is one of the boyhood homes of President Herbert Hoover, who had a Quaker upbringing. Eugene is home of the University of Oregon.

Albany's annual Timber Carnival has attracted more than 100,000 people. They view contests in all the colorful lumbering activities, such as topping out and log rolling. There is also a Parade of Logs. Forest Grove calls itself Ballad Town, U.S.A. because of its annual All Northwest Barber Shop Ballad Contest and Gay Nineties Festival. Another picturesque town is McMinnville. Without any malice, it is nicknamed The Nut City, because each year it markets millions of pounds of walnuts and filberts.

GORGEOUS GORGE

Those who drive along the scenic highway following the crest of the Columbia gorge may imagine the clumsy flatboats of the pioneers or the racing canoes of the trappers heading for old Fort Vancouver. What a different scene the mighty river presents today, enslaved by huge dams, bound by express highways, tamed by lofty bridges. And yet the grandeur discovered by the first explorers is still there.

All the way up and down the river are points of interest. At Crown Point the cathedral-like Vista House has become one of the most famous scenic trademarks in America. Multnomah Falls tumbles over its basalt cliff in a foaming drop of 620 feet (186 meters), the second highest in the United States. At Hood River, travelers may see Mount Hood thrusting its noble head above mile after mile of blooming orchards. At the Dalles, sadly, the Indians stand no more

86

with spears poised above the raging waters of Celilo Falls, waiting for salmon. The falls disappeared beneath a quiet pool when a dam was built.

Only the surgeon quarters remain at old Fort Dalles, and this has been turned into a museum, housing a rare collection of pioneer Americana. The Archaeological Museum at the Dalles also offers one of the finest collections of its kind. The Columbia has been spanned at the Dalles by a great highway bridge and dam. In the city park is the touching monument called The End of the Trail.

THE EASTERN HALF

Fossilized ancient creatures and plants are found in large numbers in many parts of the northeast section of Oregon. The town of Fossil is named for the many stony remains of nuts, leaves, and mammals that were first found there in 1876. Fossils thirty million years old are found in the Thomas Condon-John Day State Park. The park is also noted for an unusual rock formation which looks like a great cathedral. Boardman is another center for fossil collection.

The traveler who visits Pendleton during its Roundup may wonder if pioneer days have come again. A city of Indian tepees is raised, where the Indians live just as they did in the past. The annual Pendleton Roundup is one of the country's top rodeos.

Another event is the Indian Festival of Arts, at La Grande, also noted for its mineral Hot Lake. On the Grande Ronde River, daring passengers may take a ride down the swirling river from Rondowa to Troy on a rubber raft.

Wallowa Lake, surrounded by the Wallowa Mountains, is a remarkable beauty spot. Here is the region of the Nez Percé and the Chiefs Joseph. "Chief Joseph Days" are celebrated each year at Joseph in memory of the two great Indian leaders. Near Joseph is a statue erected to Old Chief Joseph. Joseph is near Eagle Gap Wilderness Area, 220,000 acres (88,000 hectares) in extent.

Not far to the east the fearsome Snake River has cut Hell's Canyon to the deepest natural gorge on the North American continent, a

thousand feet (three hundred meters) deeper than the Grand Canyon of the Colorado. Early travelers, dying of thirst, could see the great flow of the Snake River below them but had no way to get to the precious water. The boat trip through Hell's Canyon is unique. Some of the ranches in the neighborhood can be reached only by boat.

Upriver on the Snake is Brownlee Dam, second-highest rockfill dam in the world. Still farther south is Farewell Bend State Park; there travelers on the Oregon Trail said a sad farewell to the lifegiving waters of the Snake River before striking out across the wilderness.

Much of southeastern Oregon is semi-desert, with vast stretches of picturesque sage country. Wild horses still roam the range near Burns. Parts of this region are home to Basque people, who came from Spain. There are scenic wonders in this section, too. The Walls of Rome, near Rome, are a fantastic formation of fossil-bearing clay. Huge Kiger Gorge is a breathtaking, bowl-shaped hollow in the Steens Mountains. Malheur Cave is a lava cone formation ½ mile (.8 kilometer) deep, where boats are rowed on an underground lake. Malheur Wildlife Refuge is the largest in the nation—184,000 acres (74,000 hectares).

END OF THE TRAIL

The tourist business is one of the state's largest industries. Visitors add millions of dollars a year to the state's income. The trail to Oregon is no longer a difficult and dangerous one, but many a present-day traveler wishes never to leave once he has seen the land the pioneers fought so hard to reach, and many still contentedly settle down where they, too, have found "The End of the Trail."

Opposite: The Snake River is at the bottom of Hell's Canyon,
the deepest natural gorge on the North American continent.

Handy Reference Section

Instant Facts

Became the 33rd state, February 14, 1859
Capital—Salem, settled 1825
Nickname—The Beaver State
State motto—"The Union"
State animal—Beaver
State bird—Western meadowlark
State fish—Chinook salmon
State tree—Douglas fir
State flower—Oregon grape
State song—"Oregon, My Oregon"; words by J.A. Buchanan, music by
      Henry B. Murtagh
Area—96,981 square miles (251,180 square kilometers)
Rank in area—10th
Coastline—296 miles (476 kilometers)
Shoreline—1,410 miles (2,269 kilometers)
Greatest length (north to south)—290 miles (467 kilometers)
Greatest width (east to west)—375 miles (604 kilometers)
Geographic center—25 miles (40 kilometers) south-southeast of Prineville
Highest point—Mount Hood, 11,245 feet (3,427 meters)
Lowest point—Sea level
Number of counties—36
Population—2,421,000 (1980 projection)
Rank in population—31st
Population density—24.9 per square mile (9.6 per square kilometer),
      1980 projection
Rank in density—39th
Population center—In Linn County, 28 miles (45 kilometers) northeast
      of Albany
Birth rate—13.9 per 1,000
Infant mortality rate—14.9 per 1,000 births
Physicians per 100,000—154
Principal cities—Portland   379,967 (1970 census)
      Eugene   79,028
      Salem   68,480
      Corvallis   35,056
      Medford   28,454

You Have a Date with History

1543—Juan Rodríguez Cabrillo may have sighted Oregon
1603—Martin d' Augilar names Cape Blanco

1775—Bruno Heceta discovers Columbia River
1778—Captain James Cook explores coast
1792—Captain Robert Gray enters Columbia
1805—Lewis and Clark travel overland and reach Columbia mouth
1811—Pacific Fur Company establishes Astoria
1824—Dr. John McLoughlin takes charge of Oregon region at Fort Vancouver
1834—Jason and Daniel Lee establish Salem
1840—Jason Lee brings in first "large" party of settlers
1843—Informal government established; first major migration
1846—Oregon becomes American territory
1847—Cayuse War
1848—Oregon Territory established
1850—Donation Land Law
1855—Rogue River War
1859—Statehood
1864—Salem chosen by people as capital
1877—Nez Percé War
1883—Oregon opened by transcontinental railroad
1902—Initiative and Referendum laws adopted
1905—Lewis and Clark Exposition, Portland
1912—Oregon women gain right to vote
1935—State capitol destroyed by fire
1937—Bonneville Dam completed
1939—Capitol building completed at Salem
1941—Oregon National Guard first in South Pacific
1962—Storm Frieda worst ever to hit state
1964—Heavy floods damage western Oregon
1972—Nonreturnable beverage containers banned
1977—Fluorocarbon aerosol cans forbidden

Thinkers, Doers, Fighters

People of renown who have been associated with Oregon

Baker, Edward Dickinson
Balch, Frederic Homer
Bloch, Ernest
Davenport, Homer
Douglas, David
Joseph (father), Chief
Joseph (son), Chief
Lee, Daniel
Lee, Jason
Markham, Edwin
McLoughlin, John
Stackpole, Ralph
Steel, William Gladstone
Whitman, Marcus

91

Governors of the State of Oregon

John D. Whiteaker 1859-1862
A.C. Gibbs 1862-1866
George L. Woods 1866-1870
La Fayette Grover 1870-1877
Stephen F. Chadwick 1877-1878
W.W. Thayer 1878-1882
Z.F. Moody 1882-1887
Sylvester Pennoyer 1887-1895
William Paine Lord 1895-1899
T.T. Geer 1899-1903
George E. Chamberlain 1903-1909
Frank W. Benson 1909-1910
Jay R. Bowerman (acting) 1910-1911
Oswald West 1911-1915
James Withycombe 1915-1919
Ben W. Olcott 1919-1923

Walter M. Pierce 1923-1927
I.L. Patterson 1927-1929
A.W. Norblad 1929-1931
Julius Meier 1931-1935
Charles M. Martin 1935-1939
Charles A. Sprague 1939-1943
Earl Snell 1943-1947
John H. Hall 1947-1949
Douglas McKay 1949-1952
Paul L. Patterson 1952-1956
Elmo Smith 1956-1957
Robert D. Holmes 1957-1959
Mark O. Hatfield 1959-1967
Tom McCall 1967-1975
Robert W. Straub 1975-1979
Victor Atiyeh 1979-

Annual Events

February-March — All Northwest Barbershop Ballad Contest and Gay Nineties
Festival, Forest Grove
May — Azalea Festival, Brookings
June — Rose Festival, Portland
June — Indian Festival of Arts, La Grande
June — National Rooster Crowing Contest, Rogue River
June — Phil Sheridan Days, Sheridan
June — Strawberry Festival, Lebanon
July — World Championship Timber Carnival, Albany
July-August — Chief Joseph Day, Joseph
August — Regatta and Fish Festival, Astoria
August — Gold Rush Jubilee, Jacksonville
August — Scandinavian Festival, Junction City
August — Turkorama, McMinnville
September — Potato Festival, Redmond
September — Pendleton Roundup, Pendleton
Setpember — Indian Style Salmon Bake, Depoe Bay
October — Klamath Basin Potato Festival, Merrill

92

Index

94

PICTURE CREDITS

Color photographs courtesy of the following: Travel Information, Oregon State Highway Division, 10, 13, 14, 17, 21 (bottom), 25, 33, 34, 36, 40, 43, 59, 61, 67, 74, 76, 77, 79, 80, 83, 85, 88; Columbia River Maritime Museum, 8; News Bureau, University of Oregon, 18, 72; Wells Fargo Bank History Room, 64; Rasmussen Collection of Northwest Coast Indian Art, Portland Art Museum, 21 (top); USDI, NPS, Fort Clatsop National Memorial, 26; Weyerhaeuser Company, 48, 49, 56; USDI, Bureau of Reclamation, 53; Royal Ontario Museum, 54.

Illustrations on back cover by Len W. Meents.

ABOUT THE AUTHOR

With the publication of his first book for school use when he was twenty, **Allan Carpenter** began a career as an author that has spanned more than 135 books. After teaching in the public schools of Des Moines, Mr. Carpenter began his career as an educational publisher at the age of twenty-one when he founded the magazine *Teachers Digest*. In the field of educational periodicals, he was responsible for many innovations. During his many years in publishing, he has perfected a highly organized approach to handling large volumes of factual material: after extensive traveling and having collected all possible materials, he systematically reviews and organizes everything. From his apartment high in Chicago's John Hancock Building, Allan recalls, "My collection and assimilation of materials on the states and countries began before the publication of my first book." Allan is the founder of Carpenter Publishing House and of Infordata International, Inc., publishers of *Issues in Education* and *Index to U. S. Government Periodicals*. When he is not writing or traveling, his principal avocation is music. He has been the principal bassist of many symphonies, and he managed the county's leading non-professional symphony for twenty-five years.